Tibetan Society
in
Exile

Tibetan Society

in

Exile

Jayanti Alam

Raj Publications

New Delhi - 110002

Tibetan Society in Exile

First Published in 2019

ISBN 978-81-86208-12-0

₹ 795

Published by : **Raj Publications**
108, 4855/24, Ansari Road,
Daryaganj, New Delhi - 110009
Tel. : 011-23250939, 9811010939

Laser Typesetting : Aarati Computers, Delhi-110 009

Printed at : Balaji Offset, Delhi

Contents

Dedication

To My Father,
Late Moni Kanto Guha,
without whose encouragement
I could not have done anything in life.

Preface

As I was trying to understand the socio-economic conditions and the psyche of the internal or intra-regional, intra-state migrants and as I was trying to empathise with the bitter challenges and the psycho-cultural distresses they face as a result of trying to get adjusted and trying to get accepted in a totally new class/civilisational background, I started feeling almost part of them; I developed an urge to delve greater and deeper into these predicaments which these vanquished in the regional/national/international power-politics fell into and yet it was accepted as natural and inevitable. My old and continued interest and background in international relations/politics made me discover quite a few common grounds of concern and inquiries between the *intra* and *inter* national migrations. I started looking into the problems faced by the Palestinians,the Burmese, the Afghans, etc— not excluding the Bangladeshis and the Sri-Lankan Tamils. But I felt more interested in the problems of the Tibetans since I had a background in PRC's history of foreign policy with regard to those Asian countries over which pre-1949 China traditionally had or tried to have suzerain power (e.g.

Indochina/Vietnam). The second important reason that goaded me into this kind of study is my long association with the Tibetans in India—particularly those in Shimla, Dharamshala, Darjeeling and Delhi. The third and the most important reason, of course, is my deep, engaging interest in women and their existential problems from various angles and in various socio-cultural situations.

After my preliminary/background studies into (i) the Chinese version of Tibetan history, (ii) Tibetan history written by Tibetans and the Lamas actually engaged in anti-occupation struggles, by the western sympathisers and by the Indian scholars, (iii) the causes behind international migration and political asylum sought and the (iv) the over-all UN approach towards these, I went to Dharamshala (in H.P.), which was allotted by the government of India for the establishment of the Tibetans' government in exile, with His Holiness the Dalai Lama as the Head. I read important documents and interesting biographies, autobiographies, true life stories, experiences and thinkings of the Tibetan women from all socio-economic backgrounds, including those of H.H.'s sister and mother and the Tibetan Buddhist nuns. I interviewed women from all walks of life—doctors, shopkeepers, restaurant owners, teachers, librarians, receptionists, bureaucrats and simple houswives and mothers. I did start with a set questionnaire, but soon discovered that casual chatting, and discussion on the 'tete-a-tete' method was more effective. The women felt friendly and relaxed and thus, one could draw out much more from them. Several men, particularly men in political positions and husbands of successful women, were interviewed with the primary purpose of guaging the *male-bias* and *gender differences*. Both these possibilities, amagingly, were found absent. That is why, Tibetan Women's Association and other women's/nun's bodies do not really have women's problems and issues to fight or unite for.

Their chief goals and objectives are (i) Tibet's liberation and return to the motherland, (ii) *conservation* of not merely Nature and environment (along with the fiercest wild animals, etc), but also of their religion, language and culture. Till now, to my utter surprise and pleasure, I have not been able to find a single aspect/issue in their day-to-day lives where men have *more* or *different* rights than women! (iii) The Tibetan man are a firm believers in peace and harmony. That state of mind can be reached not merely by non-violence and non-belligerence but also, by non-interference.

The present study would, therefore, like to focus on the following:

(A) If the political "occupation" by Peoples' Republic of China actually destroyed oppressive feudal system and if the socio-economic condition of the common people (old serfs), and particularly women, has improved, then why did the families feel the need to migrate or leave the land, climate and environment they are so very fond of ? Why did women feel motivated to migrate when actually their socio-economic conditions were improving in their own land and they were not sure of what lay in store for them in the new land?

(B) Since, (from their own accounts and writings) the women in exile (in Dharamshala, Delhi and Shimla) are enjoying socio-economic benefits leading to gender-equality (much more than they had in pre-1951 Tibet), why is it that they still want to go back to Tibet ?

(C) Is it their deep (incomparable with any other cultural group or community) love for *undisturbed natural environment* and Tibet's very own topography, climate, flora and fauna?

(D) Or, is it because their spiritual-temporal leader, His Holiness the Dalai Lama, wants to go back and the *word* of Dalai Lama is above everythingelse—above the socio-economic benefits and the bliss of gender equality?

(E) Even if PRC leaves Tibet, what kind of socio-economic and political system the Tibetans will subscribe to since they believe that genuine freedom is attainable neither under capitalism nor under communism ?

(F) Finally, considering the gender-unequal, patriarchal Indian society around them—with which they are in constant interaction and whose over-all influence they cannot avoid—will the Tibetan society in exile be able to retain these newly-earned value-system ? Will it he easier for them to *retain* this if they get their political hold back in their motherland?

Answers to these vital questions hopefully, will enable us to look at the gender question from a new angle and thus understand this age-old problem and its possible solutions better.

My sincerest gretitude, first and foremost, goes to the great number of women in various settlements and from various walks of life, who eagerly co-operated with me in every conceivable way. The leaders of the Women's Associations and the Welfare Officers in all the settlements acted as the key force behind. I could not have progressed an inch without their able inputs in every way that was necessary. I received equal enthusiasm from the Principals, teachers and the students of the Tibetan Central Schools and the Handicrafts Centres. Hotel-owners, shop-keepers, taxi-drivers....everybody co-operated. I am specially grateful to the highly placed officials of the Tibetan government (in exile) at Dharamshala. Long stretches of interview with the P.S. to His Holiness has been specially useful and eye-opening. My observations would have been floating in the air if not for the learned assistance from the library staff at Dharamshala and the National Library at Calcutta. I could not have sorted out my observations and ideas if not for my extremely useful discussions with a few Sinologists and Tibetologists And, I may not even have got attracted towards such a study if not for my long association and cherished friendship with Dr. Tenzin Kingzyom and Dr. Sonam Lhamo (Tibetan lady doctors). I got introduced to this society because of them (particularly Dr. Tenzin Kingzyom).

Jayanti Alam

Introduction

The case of the international migrants from Tibet is something very different, distinctive, special and unique mainly because of the following striking features of this land and its people. Tibet, geographically also, is unique and distinctive.

a) The topography, climate and natural vegetation of this area calls for very hard life as well as a hard determination not merely to survive but also to live and enjoy living. This may have made the Tibetans strikingly individualistic and exclusivist.

b) Belief, genuinely, in the most fundamental message of Buddhism, viz: complete and comprehensive non-violence, or, in other words, conservation of life and environment with the sincerest commitment. The Constitution of the Tibetan government in Exile is the only known constitution that has a separate and comprehensive section on the Conservation of Nature and environment.

c) culture and custom, born out of and nurtured by this kind of religiosity and faith in the sacredness of peace, non-violence and life.

d) as a result, immense importance to religion and the institution of the Dalai Lama — in their private, social and political lives; the Dalai Lama is the temporal-cum-spiritual head, enjoined with unquestioned hold over the life and beliefs of his followers/disciples. The position of the Lamas are quite comparable to that of the Brahmins under Aryanism or Manushastra. They enjoy an authoritative position, but unlike the Brahmin priests, are not oppressive in their dealings. The day to day living and thinking of a Tibetan is almost totally guided by the local or family lamas.

e) The almost non-existent military powers of the Tibetan (Tabo) kings\warlords can be attributed to the deep belief and faith in the sacredness of peace, non-violence and life. The powerful Chinese monarchs found the spiritual impact of the Dalai Lamas more effective and lasting in their efforts to contain the "barbarian" but mighty Mongols.

f) The Tabo kings,more often than not, had a tributary relationship with the generally more powerful kings of the "Middle Kingdom"; their political power remained more on the wane as they hardly had any army or well-organized political machinery. Yet, their independent-mindedness, pride in their culture,love for life, peace and environment kept them remarkably fearless,freedom-loving and individualistic.

g) The present "democratic" constitution and the "new" gender-equal society.

Once we have clear, objective and adequate understanding of these salient features it will not be difficult to have a clear, unambiguous and non-biased picture of the present position of women in this uprooted but "newly-rooted" (if we can say so) society. It can even serve as a model for the local highly patriarchal society as well as the Indian society in its entirety. The women activists, who are endlessly struggling harder and harder for justice and equality, can very well use this model. This would put all the men in power to shame. That really is the purpose and objective of this project. A model, thus evolved, will immensely benefit both women's studies and movements; and what more can one, working for women's cause, desire and hope to achieve?

The real inspiration / motivation for this work came from my feeling that this society, unwittingly though, has succeeded in establishing a *truly* egalitarian social system, ably supported by a *truly* democratic Constitution or administrative system. I have been fortunate to be closely associated with this community for the past 20 years or so having lived in Himachal Pradesh and having been a beneficiary of their medical system. This State is strewn with Tibetan settlements all over; and the space for the Tibetan government in exile has been provided in McLeodganj near Dharamshala (in Himachal Pradesh). As a crusader for equality and women / human / natural rights, I further, felt that this "new-born" society can serve as an apt *model* for any society struggling to break the chains of age-old inequalities, caused by the concentration of wealth and power in the hands of a few unscrupulous males. This, really, is the purpose of this project.

The foundations on which my work started initially were:

(i) the impression that I gathered as a result of my long and close association with the Tibetan lady doctors in exile (through whom I initially got introduced to this society),

(ii) the lasting impression that I carried from my childhood (due to my friendship with the pre-1959 Tibetans in the Darjeeling district of West Bengal),

(iii) extensive reading of research & anecdotal books, written by the Tibetans, Tibetologists and even travelers.

It was also necessary to acquaint myself, briefly though, with the political & cultural history of the bi-lateral, as well as tripartite relations among the three countries, viz: India, China and Tibet. But, the most important plank was the tete-a-tete with the women & girls of various ages and occupations from various camps and settlements, spread over a few settlements of the Himalayan India and also Delhi. Large meetings used to be arranged by the Tibetan Women's Associations or/ and the Tibetan Welfare Officers and these encounters used to go on till even after dinner-time—the enthusiasm used to be so great on their part. I made it a point to talk to every single Tibetan woman/ girl that I came across—on the roads, in the shops/ restaurants/ hotels, in offices, libraries, schools,etc. I made special visits to the Tibetan Central Schools, opened by the Government of India, and had extremely useful interactions with the teachers, the students, the clerical staff and the Principal. I talked to the pious women in the "goomphas" and during the special New Year and Kalachakra functions. These provided me with good opportunities to talk to men, children and also those who belonged to the grandparents' generation. I talked, at length, to the housewives also.

We must note, in this context, that

(i) no Tibetan woman is a full-fledged housewife the way we understand in the mainstream Indian culture; almost all women are fruitfully engaged in some business or the other, and

(ii) all women—however busy she may be in her occupation or livelihood activity— devote a good amount of time to housekeeping, and specially to taking adequate care of the young and the old.

(iii) motherhood is the greatest and most essential virtue of a woman in both Tibetan culture and Buddhism.

(iv) woman's work, both at home and outside, is equally, and *willingly* shared by men, and the family (comprising of three generations) works as a unit according to individual capabilities, and takes decisions as a unit.

A substantial number of men — various government officials, including His Holiness' Private Secretary, Welfare Offices, bus-drivers, taxi-drivers, porters, etc.—offered remarkably eager co-operation. In majority of the cases, I was happily helped by the interpreters, voluntarily done even by the taxi-drivers. In short, the co-operation and enthusiasm among all sections of Tibetans was much more than expected. A very small number of the very rich, who emotionally miss the "good old days" of the British imperialism and welcome the neo-imperialism of globalization or the world-wide trend of market-economy, were the exceptions.

The camps/ settlements visited by me were in Dharamshala, H.P. (the headquarters of the Tibetan Government-in-exile), Shimla, Delhi,and various towns and small towns of the Darjeeling district. I was scheduled to visit two camps in Arunachal Pradesh also, but could not make it due to rail & road disruptions by the Bodo militants in the areas leading to these settlements. I may be accused of ignoring the South (Karnataka), where the first and the largest settlements are found. But the primary purpose of my field visits was to investigate into the possible causes behind such dramatically radical changes found in the new societies that have taken roots in the Indian soil. For that, it was advisable to confine my studies to the similar topographical, climatic & cultural zones. The time constraint was also important.

It was absolutely necessary to study the Constitution of the Government-in-exile and talk to the officials and the members of their Parliament. I needed a relaxed time with the Tibetans who have been residing in India since many generations. Their forefathers had migrated to the Darjeeling district as traders & merchants. They consider themselves Indians, and they have Indian citizenships and jobs (even in the Indian Defence Services)...This survey of/interaction with the "Indian" Tibetans was the most beneficial since I felt that I discovered the "source" of inspiration behind the amazing gender-equality in their new society (in exile).

The method of using structured questionnaire— a method generally followed in these kind of studies— was not found useful and had to be discarded totally because the majority of the interviewees/ respondents felt stiff and closed up in front of a tape recorder or an array of formal questions. In fact, they did not like questions at all. Useful and interesting information had to be culled out of casual, informal conversations over tea, dinner, shopping or religious ceremonies. May be only ten out of a hundred sentences spoken were relevant for the purpose of the present study. Yet, listening to a hundred was necessary and important.

The questionnaire method did not work even with the educated groups like teachers, students, bureaucrats, etc.—not because they felt stiff or withdrawn, but because they went down their memory lanes and would not stop rumbling. The first few questions triggered off so much in them that there was no scope left (for me) to ask any more questions. The trauma of they having been thrown out of their hearth and home has made some of them withdrawn and suspicious....But, at the same time, they take very little time in opening up and being helpful once they feel our sympathy and concern. They felt that I was identifying with their cause.

As a student of International Relations, with specialization in Chinese Studies, I found it necessary to understand the role and attitude of PRC with regard to its "occupation" of Tibet. So, I tapped the Chinese sources to study the problem from the PRC angle.

The total elimination of feudalism and the lessening, if not eradication, of class divisions had already prepared the grounds for women's rights in TAR (Tibetan Autonomous Region). The new found gender equality in the Tibetan society in exile may have been because of the impressions the migrants carried from TAR. Or, because of the real life stories and information they keep getting from their friends and relatives who have stayed back. The Dalai Lama and other political leaders and the Parliamentarians too, might have been influenced by the encouraging features of the PRC framework in post-1951 Tibet.

I have also fallen back on the books written and the reports and videos prepared by the Indian scholars and travelers. It is very difficult for a photograph or a video to tell lies or cook up stories. An a-political traveler also is not likely to do that....So, they tell us a lot about the real picture of "progress", "modernization" and "freedom" in China-"occupied" Tibet. [Quotation marks have been used with words which are controversial and constitute the bone of contention between the Tibetan refugees and the government in their land which they have left.]

I had extensive discussions with the Tibetologists, Sinologists and other Indian scholars and was in constant touch with Indo-Tibet Friendship Society,both at McLeodganj and New Delhi.

I had also found it necessary and worthwhile to talk to the Chinese residents of India in order to get an idea of what their forefathers thought, felt and were told about the social and political status of "independent" Tibet. This made the understanding of the Chinese views on Tibet and China's role in Tibet much more objective. I chose Calcutta for this purpose since the Chinese there are largest in number and oldest by way of residence.

A comprehensive review of literature did not become possible since I could not locate a single study, preceding mine, on this problem. I could not succeed even after scanning through the footnotes, the end notes and the references in the books that I studied.

II

The present study is of the Tibetan society in exile (India) with special attention to the position or the socio-economic condition of these women. The purpose is to project this society as a model for gender equality so that the women and the activists of India and other parts of the world can motivate their own society, towards gender equity.

We shall notice, as we go ahead with our study, that this kind of radical transformation may not have (or, could not have) taken place without a radical shift in the socio-political situation in Tibet. This may not have been caused by the Chinese Communist occupation of Tibet, but did definitely happen **after** the occupation and **after** the lamas, headed by Dalai Lama, lost their temporal powers. Studied from this angle, the issue has strong political dimensions. That is why, Chapter I has to look, briefly though, into the political history of relations among the three civilizations and power-players, viz: China, India and Tibet.

Since the year of Chinese occupation (1951) serves as a watershed between a backward feudal society and a social-democratic polity, it is essential to have an idea of the pre-1951 Tibet. We must try to understand:

(i) to what extent pre-1951 affected post-1951 and particularly, post-1959 (the year they fled to India)

(ii) to what extent post-1951/ 1959 is a radical change on pre-1951

(iii) is the said model society a result of (a) post-1951, (b) post-1951 cum 1959, or just (c) post-1959

Our understanding and assessment of the present society in exile would be in vacuum unless and until we are aware of the features of the pre-modern Tibetan society. This justifies the writing of the second chapter.

Buddhism shows the path to tolerance and non-violence. I do not mean that the other religions preach violence, but no other religion lays so much of emphasis on peace and non-violence as the **one and the only** mode of life and living. Buddhism had spread to so many other parts of South, East and South-east Asia; there was Buddhism in China also. But nowhere-else has it played such a dominant role, lasting to this day in its fullest glory. It will be, therefore, a lopsided or incomplete understanding of the Tibetan society and psyche if we do not try to get a clear picture of Buddhism, Tibetan Buddhism and Lamaism (Chapter III).

All cultural traits and trends and even strong foundations like religious beliefs undergo change and develop its own peculiarities/ characteristics, depending on the geographical, social and political factors of a particular time and place. The institution of the lamas (the religious teachers) and their role in the day to day lives of the Tibetan people is worth a special attention in our attempt to understand the society.The role of the lamas and the people's deep emotional attachment to His Holiness the Dalai Lama have remained the same notwithstanding their democratic-socialist Constitution. There has been a revolutionary transformation in their thinking and living. In its attitudes and behaviour this society is more secular than the 'declared' secular polity of India. The society does not contain even traces of authoritarianism and patriarchy, though a typical religious society cannot really be free of these malaise. This is another reason why I got attracted to a study of this society.

The nearest comparison of the institution of the Dalai lama can be, perhaps, with the Pope or with the four

Shankaracharyas. He is the spiritual cum temporal mentor/ leader of all Tibetans—in whichever part of the globe they may be residing. But, the present Dalai Lama, unlike the Pope, is extremely secular and a true, practicing believer in democracy. He even advocates the abolition of the very institution of the Dalai Lama (i) when people want so and/ or (ii) when the Tibetans go back to their own land and establish democracy, socialism and secularism. Unlike the Shankaracharyas, the Dalai Lama is not at all authoritarian and obscurantist. He genuinely believes in peace, democracy and science-based progress— or whatever is good for his people. Chapters III and IV of this study are devoted to an understanding and analysis of these.

I failed to arrive at a clear conclusion regarding what contributed to or generated such a gender equal society, which I have tried to portray as a model. Apparently, it is the democratic Constitution of the Tibetan government in exile. But, I have also discussed in my chapters the possible influence of and inspiration from (i) the socialist reforms, laws and policies in TAR and/ or (ii) the gender equal society that already existed among the pre-1959 migrants in the Darjeeling district of West Bengal.

That is why a somewhat detailed analysis of the major provisions of the Tibetan Constitution became necessary in Chapter V. This Constitution is more or less a copy of the Indian Constitution. The major difference is in the fact that the former has a separate section on the conservation of Nature and environment. Strangely but, our own Constitution has not been able to inspire the people to the high ideals that its makers had so painstakingly laid down. It could not achieve, in half a century, what its copy did in just 40 years. How many more years we have to travel to become truly democratic, socialist and secular? In such a division-less society—if at all— gender discrimination too, will not be able to persist.

We need to inquire, at this stage, is the Constitution a reflection of a society's thoughts and aspirations, or the society gets moulded, and remoulded, in the lines set by the Constitution. In the case of the Tibetans may be both are true.

Chapters VI and VII contain the main body of my arguments, based purely on my interviews, conversations and discussions. These are the outcomes of my grand experience which I shall cherish for the rest of my academic, activist and personal life.

The last chapter, viz: VIII, is an attempt at a recap or a reminder of the features which are striking and exceptional and because of which the Tibetan Society in Exile can be admired as a model in gender equality and equity. The Conclusion follows from this.

1

Historical Background

Let us start at the very beginning i.e. delve, very 'briefly, into the history of (a) Sino-Tibet, (b) Indo-Tibet and (c) Sino-Indian relations. Our focus will be on the period when the institution of the Dalai Lama got imposed and, subsequently accepted, as the most crucial factor in the evolution of Tibetan thought, society and psyche. This has remained as important and as significant to this day. This, undoubtedly, is a feature unique to this society. Can we think of any civilization where the same streak continues over many centuries notwithstanding many noteworthy changes in political power as well as in the living pattern and the thought-processes of its people? Deep and unshakable reverence to the Dalai Lama and its institution continues undiluted inspite of the remarkable dynamism towards modernization, democratization and,above all, gender-equity.

Sino-Tibet Relations

According to a stone inscription, belonging to the 8th century, and also according to the Lama historians, Spu-rgyal was the first-known Tibetan king. It is fondly believed that this first in the line was the son of an Indian king, related to Lord Buddha; and with him came the end of Bon-po or the Bon religion and the beginning of Buddhism. The first seven hereditary (primogeniture) kings are called "the heavenly thrones". They were believed to have descended from heaven by a celestial rope,which helped them to ascend back to the sky after their death.[1] See, how the "holy" and the "unquestionable" concept of the Dalai Lama has its origin in this legend/myth. It is important to note, in this connection, that the Tibetans firmly believe that the parental blood continues to flow down to the seventh generation in case of both matrilineal and patrilineal descent. Therefore, one can marry in one's own clan only in the eighth generation.[2] Twenty-seven or more kings ruled this mystic land after the initial" heavenly seven", and they were classified as" Earthly" and "Human".[3] This is an admission of the reality or the inevitability of the gradual decline in quality/virtue/ heavenliness when the rulers are not supernatural and the kingdom is not outside the boundaries of the earth.

Padmasambhava and Shantirakshita, great Buddhist scholars of India,had been invited to Tibet to import and impart Vajrayana version of Buddhism around 747 A.D.[4] Vajrayana is Buddhism tainted by certain beliefs and rites of the Tantrics. It became easier to drive away the "barbaric" Bon-po religion/rituals because of the powerful presence of Tantra in this version of Buddhism. (Supernatural beliefs of the pre-Buddhist Bon Po faith was termed barbaric. But the Tantric rites, imported from non-Buddhist India, were no less superstitious, if not barbaric.) Pure theory/ethics of Buddhism would have appeared too unworldly and the people would have felt,kind of, anchorless.

The Words Of My Perfect Teacher was a kind of Geeta or Quoran for the Dharma-loving Tibetans. It talks of Tibetan mythology. During the time of Buddha Tibet had no human inhabitants. Later it got inhabited by descendants of an ape (an emanation of the noble Avalokiteshvara) and a crag-demoness (believed to be an emanation of goddess Tara). Tibet was in a state of chaos, with no religion, no laws and no ruler at its head. Meanwhile, in India a deformed son was born to a king called Shatanika. He was banished as he was feared to be non-human or sub-human. His wanderings ended up in Tibet, where he met a group of shepherds. When they asked him where he came from he is said to have pointed to the sky. The god-fearing shepherds took him to be a god since he resided above them. They instantly made him their chief.[5] Thus, the very first ruler or king of Tibet was believed to be from India. Not only that, this king was revered as a manifestation of divine Bodhisattva Sarva-nivarana-vishkambhin.

Five generations later, in the beginning of the 7th. cent., came the reign of Songsten Gampo—also an emanation of Avalokiteshvara. He took, in marriage, the Chinese princess Kongjo (an emanation of goddess Tara) and a Nepalese princess Tritsun (a manifestation of the goddess Bhrikuti). Each brought with her, as a part of dowry, an image of Lord Buddha.[6] Such myths and legends, which are in no mean number in Tibet, show clearly the pre-historic and historic links and influences that these neighbouring civilizations had on Tibet. For the first time, during this period, Tibetan alphabet was introduced by Thonmi Sambhota. He also studied languages under an Indian Pandit (scholar) named Devajit Singha...The "supernatural" king manifested a monk, named Akarmti, from in between his eye-brows, who went to convert the non-Buddhist kings of India.[7] These kinds of informations, even if based more on beliefs and legends than on researched history, are useful reiteration of the facts that cultural relations/ influences between Tibet and India were ancient, firm and lasting and that these were both historical and historic.

King Songsten Gampo is remembered specially for

having unified the various Tibetan tribes scattered over a vast area.[8] Yet, he continued to have good relations with the Tang dynasty of China. According to writings on the stone-pillars, in both Tibetan & Chinese scripts in both Lhasa and the then Chinese capital Chang'an, Tibet (between 7th.& mid-9th. cent.) was a strong, independent and expansionist power[9] and a serious rival to China in the region of Central Asia. Its influence extended across the Pamirs upto the empires of the Arabs and the Turks in the west, over Turkestan in the north and Nepal in the south and most important of all—in the east upto Gansu and large parts of Sichuan. The Tibetan army exacted an yearly tribute from China.[10] Some accounts claim that Tibet even took over the Chinese capital, Chang'an in, 763 A.D.[11]

During the 13th. century Tibet had been ruled by various war-lords. China too, during most of the feudal or pre-revolution period, experienced the supremacy of the warlords. This was because of extremely weak monarchy. It is important to mention here that the real reason behind China giving a great deal of importance to Tibet and the Dalai Lamas in this period, was to contain the fearsome Mongols with the spiritual influence of the Dalai Lamas.They not only preached the sacredness of peace and life, but actually meant it and believed in it. Their preachings had an effective impact even on the war-mongering, violence-loving Mongols.[12] The Chinese rulers had the right perception and wisdom and,therefore, found it wise not to alienate the Tibetan kings and people; but, at the same time, they did not allow the expansion of Tibetan political power beyond a controllable form. In any case, that kind of expansion of Tibetan power was not possible also. Due to its tradition of complete non-violence, utter absence of avarice and indestructible blind faith in Lamaism, Tibet did not build any military power.

This appears to be quite similar to the pre-historic

Indus Valley civilizations. It is interesting to note, in this context, that the Tibetan civilization was as developed in art and craft, town-planning, etc. It was highly developed in astrology, medicine and environment-science/management also.[13] Though the first two, viz: astrology and medicine, had originally traveled from India, they came back to modern India in a much developed form after the mass-scale immigration of the Tibetans. It has become a saviour of all those patients with whom Allopathy or Homeopathy have failed. These are the benefits/boons of peace, which gives leisure and peace of mind—absolutely essential for any work of art or serious philosophical and intellectual persuasion. The resultant absence of social divisions, discriminations and conflict could have also prepared the ground for gender and class equities.

War and violence are born out of intolerance and hatred and, in turn, create hatred and division in the society. The Tibetans have continued to remain, over the centuries, a cohesive group, though now spread over an extremely vast geo-climatic area. They are proud,emotional, conservative and exclusivist about their religion; traditions and culture. They have always felt helpless vis-a-vis any military prowess. More often than not,that is why,the Chinese rulers succeeded in keeping the Tabo or the Tibetan rulers tied down to a position of "tributary".[14] But,as mentioned earlier, the Chinese rulers could not afford not to have a friendly or conciliatory approach, as the good offices of the Dalai Lamas were very much necessary to contain the Mongols effectively....It is worth mentioning here (though not totally contextual) that their life in exile,though full of deep emotional disturbances and tension due to not being able to achieve freedom for their most beloved motherland, is quite smooth, tension-less and even contented because of this important factor.

The practice of maintaining a spiritual lineage of the

lamas through reincarnation arose in the 14th. century when Karma-pa proclaimed (1284-1338) that he would be reborn as re-incarnation. The third in the lineage, Bsod-nams-rgya-mtso (1543-88), was invited to Mongolia by Altan Khan. The latter was the first of the Mongols to be greatly impressed by this lama and conferred on him the title of Dalai Lama in 1578. Talai(Dalai), in his language, meant "ocean", thus signifying the vast and deep wisdom of the lama.[15] The Tibetans do not address the Dalai Lama by the title but as Yid-bzhin Norbu-bu, meaning "wish-granting jewel", or as Rgyul-ba Rin-po-che,meaning "great precious conqueror"; at present he is referred to as His Holiness.[16] In a short time, the other lamas also started commanding the spiritual allegiance of all the rival tribes of Mongolia.[17] The supreme allegiance to Dalai Lama led to the unification of the Mongol empire; but,at the same time this contributed to the toning down of the aggressive temperament of the Mongols. Gushri Khan assumed the title "king of Tibet" and took special interest in and responsibility of protecting the "kingdom of the Dalai Lama". He maintained friendly and respectful relations with the Dalai Lama on the one hand, and took every care to keep a check on the latter's supremacy, on the other, After his death in 1655,his successors showed little interest in their control over Tibet; they appointed a regent to attend to the minimum formalities.[18]

The 5th. Dalai Lama showed the right kind of interest, determination and courage to draw all powers into his own hands, including that of the appointment of the regent. This unnerved the Chinese rulers. This is a significant landmark in the history of Sino-Tibetan relations. China started realising the culture-specific undeniable importance of the Dalai Lama and that the Tibetans could not be won over or ruled over without due respect being paid to this unique institution or cultural symbol. In 1659, Dayan Khan, the Mongol king, helped 5th Dalai Lama to suppress a revolt in Tsang.[19] "The

Great Fifth", as he was known in admiration, united entire Tibet. The last time Tibet had been unified like this was by a pre-Buddhism king, follower of Bon-po religion, (which was regarded as the religion of the barbarians by the Buddhists or the later Tibetans). So he was invited by the then Manchu emperor and Tibet was accorded the official recognition of an "independent sovereign country".

The Tibetan landlords had called the king of Turkestan to defeat the Mongol king, who was trying to protect the 6th.Dalai Lama from the wrath of the common people...they were extremely agitated against him because he had been found writing love-poems.[20] China reacted at once to the "audacity" of the Tibetans and dispatched an army which entered Lhasa in 1720. The 7th.Dalai Lama was recognised as incarnate and enthroned at the Potala (by the Chinese).[21] They showed off their military strength and the extent of imperialist authority over Tibet by pulling down the walls of Lhasa and by installing a garrison there; China's representatives were posted throughout eastern Tibet and, of course, Lhasa. Ever since, Tibet continued to remain under the military supervision and suzerainty of China. At the same time, the Chinese were wise enough to accept the very special position of the Dalai Lama as the supreme ruler of his land and people.

About the middle of the 19th.century the political power of China, as we all know,was very much on the decline. The sun of the British Empire was then shining brightly on the major parts of Asia and Africa. So, Tibet started raising its head and defying Chinese claim that Tibet always 'was and is' part of China. The British, as expected, took advantage of this political situation and entered into a treaty with China, proposing the opening of the Tibetan territory to British trade. Tibet was greatly agitated and opposed this foreign interference tooth and nail. In 1894, the 13th. Dalai Lama came to the throne. He was only eighteen, but was clever and mature enough to realise that the best ally in this kind of a political game (of the British) was Russia.[22]

The British, first, tried to appease Tibet. Lord Curzon wrote in his letter to the Secretary of State for India, that "the Chinese suzerainty over Tibet is a constitutional fiction, a political affection ....Dalai Lama is the de facto as well as the de jure sovereign of the country." But he soon took the path of oppression and suppression when Tibet did not concede. In 1903, Col. Younghusband led a military expedition to Tibet and the Dalai Lama had to run away to Mongolia. In 1906-7, a treaty, conferring trade rights to the British in Tibet, was signed between Britain and China. Russia,at this stage, was not powerful enough to help or protect Tibet; it,on the contrary, signed a treaty with Britain.[23] China availed of this golden opportunity to bring Tibet back into her fold ;she invited the Dalai Lama, who was thoroughly disgruntled with Russia—China's political rival. The Dalai Lama had no other option but to welcome this and take shelter. The Dalai Lama could, thus, return to Potala in 1909 after 5 years of exile ,but had to again go in exile— this time to India[24]— the very next year because China could not desist herself from her age-old practice of keeping her thumb firm on this peace-loving, army-less, freedom-loving nation.

Tibet was not allowed to enjoy freedom even after the Revolution of 1911 which was purportedly meant to bring freedom to the common people of China. It tried to propagate the anti-imperialist and pro-republican ideas and ideologies. But,nothing really changed in favour of people.This, unfortunately, is the unending and unchanging story of "power"— whether under monarchy, feudalism or "people's" government. Has the democratic republic of India been able to understand/ accept the vital question of "identity" within its multi-racial, multi-cultural polity ? Have the parties in power been able to grant/ concede autonomy to Kashmir, North-east, Telengana, Jharkhannd or Uttarakhand, for example ? Within a year, in 1912 itself, the Republic of China proclaimed Tibet to be a province of China and troops were dispatched to ensure that.[25] In 1913, a tripartite conference among Britain, China and Tibet insisted that Chinese suzerainty over Tibet be accepted, though Tibet cannot be a province of China. Outer Tibet was to be recognized as fully autonomous, but inner Tibet was to be jointly administered by both Tibet and China.[26] The latter refused to accede, and the former, more or less, functioned independent with British support.(Everybody knows how weak China was under Kuo-min-tang,though it had managed to overthrow the Manchus and the feudal warlords for the first time in Chinese history.)

Real trouble started for the Tibetans when the Communists came to power. They were not weak like their predecessors and they wanted power and influence over as vast a territory and as big a population as it could be possible. This was the compulsion of their ideology; political power, for them, was the most effective tool/means to the goal of spreading ideology. Tibet, due to its long history of more or less submissive /tributary relationship with China, was therefore, the softest target for this kind of "missionary" zeal. Talks were arranged one after another in the "neutral" territories of Hong Kong and Delhi. As expected, nothing concrete came out in favour of Tibet. Finally, the talks shifted to the Chinese capital itself and on 24th. October,1950, one year after the establishment of "Peoples' Republic", China ordered the "Peoples' Liberation Army" (PLA) "to advance into Tibet to liberate 3 million Tibetans from imperialistic rule" [Report of the International Commission of Jurists, 1959].

In a desperate appeal to the U N, Dalai Lama's

government tried to impress upon the comity of nations that it should intervene on Tibet's behalf. It gave special emphasis to the point that one kind of oppression (viz: oppression by feudalism) cannot possibly be checked or done away with by another kind of oppression (viz: PRC's military occupation and torture). Nothing much could come out of the discussions since two Big powers, viz: USSR and PRC, strongly opposed Tibet's viewpoint and another Big power, USA, agreed to India's suggestion for a "peaceful and honourable settlement". So the "liberation" campaign of the PLA, aided by the Chinese administrative, educational and technological personnel posted in Tibet, continued in full vigour while the Tibetans continued to feel threatened by this "aggression" on their culture.[27] As mentioned earlier, the Tibetans find themselves closest to India culturally since Buddhism had traveled from India.[27a] This feeling/thinking can be considered valid. Loss of political power, to them, meant loss of cultural/religious freedom, as if. But the landless and rightsless commoners of the old system who had no 'power' of whatever kind, must have welcomed the "division-less" /privilege-less system brought in by this new power structure. In exile their government has introduced similar classless eco-political system and they are enjoying this new-found freedom and relative affluence, as a result. This radically new socio-political system has ensured gender-equality and gender-power.

As a contrast to the PRC policy in Tibet, we are tempted to look into the basic principles of the Panchashila, signed at the regional co-operation conference at Bandung in Indonesia (1955). They were (1) mutual respect for territorial integrity and sovereignty, (2) non-aggression, (3) non-interference in internal matters, (4) equality and mutual benefit and (5) peaceful co-existence. Once again, we are left with no other option but to lament at the questionable morality of the players of political game—national and international. PRC violated all the promises of the Panchashila. Not that India or the other signatories behaved any better. Subjugation is a necessary rung to power-ladder....Will it sound too incontextual if we compare this duplicity with the typical behaviour of a Hindu husband, who takes numerous vows of "life together", i.e. sharing pleasures and duties of married life and allowing her equal position in every minute sphere of life ahead but, in reality, does exactly the opposite? This, quite, is the nature of any power-game—domestic, regional,national or international. Power, whether caste, class or gender-based, cannot possibly survive unless founded on a rigid division of the society into the 'depriver' and the 'deprived', where the deprived gets more and more deprived till the equation is 100:0. It is at this point of seemingly "no return" that the have-not suddenly raises its head and turns the table completely on the have or the oppressor. Hope and values would have been dead words if not for this inevitable process—whatever the time-frame.

However ambitious the leaders of "people's" China might have been,they had the right kind of wisdom /vision born out of their long experience with peoples' miseries and aspirations; they also had the confidence born out of the success of the "long march" and the revolution. That is why Marshall Chen Yi, Dy. Prime Minister, who was assigned the task of preparing Tibet for a regional autonomy within the PRC, publicly said in April,1956, "both the Chinese government and the Communist Party held the view that reforms in Tibet can only be carried out when the Tibetan leaders & people unanimously demanded them." The preparatory committee for Tibetan Autonomous Region (TAR) was formed with Dalai Lama as its Chairman & Panchen Lama as its Vice-Chairman.[28]

The Tibetans were no fools—not particularly the educated gentry and the upper strata of the society; they joined the so-called peoples' revolt. If we go into the details of the cultural history of Tibet and particularly, into the socio-economic structure (viz: land and therefore, power concentrated in the hands of monasteries & nobility), we have every reason to believe that the staunch opposition to the socialistic reforms got engineered by that section of society which faced total loss of power & property as a result of the extension of the Chinese revolution. This was done in a restrained manner so that strong religious sensibilities of the Tibetans did not get too disturbed. No sequence of events or historical evidence from the period 1951 to 1959 explains why Dalai Lama & his supporters did not run away in 1951 itself. There is no clear evidence to show that the Chinese became suddenly more oppressive or intolerant after 8 long years.[29] On the contrary, it is natural and happens more often than not that the first onslaught comes as a real shock and the people resist it with spontaneous zest & vigour, but, over a period of time, they start getting accustomed and even start accepting. They may even start seeing the good or beneficial points....The Tibetan commoners were no exception (as Chapter VIII will show).

According to a few scholarly Tibetans, PRC's campaign for occupation started (in 1950) from the Kham province in the North, proceeded to Amdo in the East, facing continuous and determined resistance from the people everywhere. It was as late as in 1954 that PLA managed to occupy the centre of Tibetan political power, viz: Lhasa. There were a series of negotiations—17 point negotiations—till the entire effort collapsed in 1959, when DL was left with no other option but to run away.[30]

A typical Tibetan characteristic is blind faith in and deep regard for the lamas, particularly the Dalai Lama. But, this does not stop them from admitting that in exile, for the first time in their history, there was secular education for all, irrespective of class & gender, and there were job opportunities & avenues for income for all who got the necessary education & training, irrespective, once again, of class & gender. They could not dream of all these while in Tibet. Long, informal "chit-chat" suddenly puts them off-guard and they start talking about the benefits of modern (or secular) education for all, which necessarily diminishes the old class & gender differences and demolishes the rigidities of do's & don'ts,taboos & rituals—thus opening up opportunities for varieties of jobs, higher income, etc. What is more important is that the new system offered one the freedom to take decisions about one's own life. In their own admission, the Tibetans, particularly the women, are very happy with their life here,in exile; they are extremely grateful to the Government of India for providing them with an "excellent" system of education (as well as avenues for income) which they could not have even dreamt of in their own country. Nevertheless,they vehemently deny the fact that PRC "occupation" had also opened up same or similar avenues for them. If pinned down to that, they, loaded with emotions, start accusing China of "destroying their rich culture, imposing anti-religious communist value-system, education through a foreign,viz:Chinese, language and, of course, inhuman torture and repression".[31] They, accuse the Chinese of thrusting an education system which has no relation or relevance to their life-situation.[32] They overlook the fact that in India (or in any other country where they have taken refuge) the medium of instruction is not Tibetan language and some of the Tibetans even choose not to go to a Tibetan school. With the opening up of the world to them, because of universal modern education and a "welcome" sign from the West, the Tibetans, including women, have become highly ambitious and aspiring. So, they fully realise the tremendous benefits of English language and Western education. I have met a good number of young girl students who came to India not from TAR as refugees, but to learn the English language better.

The Tibetans, particularly the women, clearly do not want to give up the socio-economic benefits and freedom, that they have earned, curiously, after having left the land for whose freedom they are clamouring and even inflicting self-torture! The voice of his people was heard and understood by Dalai Lama. So, a radical Constitution was written, copying India's.[32] They cherish the idea of returning to their motherland, establish to the new socio-political structure sanctioned by this Constitution....A very significant question that we can ask here is would the Tibetans have got this new life, personal /individual freedom and a democratic /radical power-structure if the guardians of feudalism were not driven out of their land and power?

II

The main reason apparently, for the flight of Dalai Lama, along with his followers, the lamas and the nobility, was as follows:- On March 9,1959 Dalai Lama received an invitation from the Commander at Lhasa to present himself at the Chinese barracks. It was made mandatory in the invitation that he should not be accompanied by his ministers and the usual escorts. This created an additional fear and suspicion among his coterie.[33] This was found to be a good occasion to pass on the fear and suspicion to the credulous masses who, already were fed with the powerful theory that the PRC occupation had been with the sole purpose of annihilating the great Tibetan civilization. They were also made to believe that whatever the Chinese did —even if it were introducing modern education and technological advancements—was with that aim only. This, no doubt, was the surest way of continuing to weild 'the authority' which had been dealt a severe blow by the Chinese occupation. People of Lhasa, of all classes and ranks, flooded into the grounds of Norbu Lingua and outside. The Chinese, naturally, had to take very strong steps to curb or quell the rebellion; they fired two shells on this ground, close to Dalai Lama's palace, on March, 17,1959. The panic-stricken Tibetans wanted their supreme leader to run to safety, and India, due to geographical & cultural proximity, was found to be the best bet. His Holiness started his arduous journey on March 17th. itself.[34]

The monks and the dispossessed feudal lords were the most eager flight-companions since they had lost everything they had and there did not appear to be any possibility of regaining those in the near future; they lived under the constant fear of being further humiliated and disgraced. They wanted this panic-flight to look less obtrusive. So they cleverly doused the masses into a kind of xenophobia. They were made to blindly follow their ex-lords out of the "hell" that was created out of their "beloved" motherland due to the Chinese "aggression".[35]

According to Dalai Lama, China attacked Tibet due to three main reasons—(1) to accommodate China's very big population in the vast expanse of Tibet, (2) to exploit the rich mineral resources of Tibet and (3) to dominate Tibet because that was an important step towards the domination of the rest of Asia.[36] The argument that China offered was "liberation" of as many people and as many countries "languishing" under "oppressive" feudalism and monarchy.[37] We all know that Vietnam had offered a similar argument when it launched a massive offensive against Khmer Rouge tyranny in Kampuchea. In such a situation one has to decide whether norms of international relations /politics is more important than basic human rights, values and issues.

About 80,000 refugees fled to India, via Nepal & Bhutan and also to Nepal & Bhutan themselves, initially in 1959, and the flight continues ever since.[38] This continuation is a rather intriguing fact as one fails to understand what 'new' or 'more oppressive' thing kept happening in PRC-occupied Tibet for people to migrate after so many years of the "invasion /occupation"! All kinds of reports from all types of research & international bodies, even from the anti-China & pro-Tibet sources, indicate that China became accommodating and understanding over the years; they, even, realised and rectified some of their mistakes /excesses, particularly those committed during the "Cultural Revolution".[39] So, if the Tibetans could take the initial "attack", (which was really harsh, by all accounts—even the Chinese later realised and admitted), then why was it that they could not adjust /accept when things were not too bad for them? (1) Was it because they kept hoping that they will be able to see the end of the tunnel soon,i.e. India and the world body will be able to convince or force China to status quo? So, they waited in TAR for a while (2) Was it that they were able to perceive the benefits of the reforms & innovations brought about by PRC and was therefore, waiting in Tibetan Autonomous Region itself to see better days? Or,(3) was it that they were lured by the encouraging reports they kept receiving from their friends and relatives who were enjoying the fruits of parliamentary democracy put into effect by the Dalai Lama's government-in-exile?

III

As mentioned earlier, the Tibetan commoners, living in India, are very happy with their new society which is marked by gender-equality and the near absence of class difference and hierarchy. This feeling of happiness is much more pronounced among the women who have migrated and have, thus, experienced and seen both sides of the Himalayas, or both types of lives, viz: under pre- modern feudo-monastic socio- economic system, on the one side, and under bourgeois-democratic structure, on the other. Quite a few of them were also in the enviable position of comparing and judging the pros & cons of both the "reforms", viz: by the Chinese in Tibet and by the Tibetan government-in-exile.....Interestingly, but, young Tibetan women, born in India and having no first-hand information or experience of what was life in Tibet before and after the Chinese occupation, seem to be more enthusiastic and emotional about freeing their motherland and returning. This generation, otherwise, has totally & completely taken to modern Western learning and life-style and has also imbibed the Western secular values very well. Quite a few of them do not even know how to read & write their own language (all of them, of course, can and do speak), wear modern /Western dresses and prefer West to India or Tibet. Study of many a community in peril shows that patriotism or nationalist feelings,purely at the level of values, concept and imagination, tend to be chauvinistic or, even, xenophobic, as patriotism is usually a "tutored" belief or an imbibed "emotion". A major part of Hindu India is becoming a victim of this kind of patriotism.....But, the love of the modern young Tibetans for their cultural uniqueness—e.g. dance, music, food, etc.—is genuine; not like in case of "Hindutva" conscious upper class Indians.

The refugees strongly feel that they have lost their motherland due to their bad deeds or the working of the evil spirits. Lord Buddha, as one of the ten "avtars"/ incarnations of "Puranic" beliefs, was as much a strong believer in the theory of Karma as any normal God-fearing Hindu is. One fails to understand how can there be a collective bad deed! The theory of Karma talks of *individual* good or bad deeds and their effects on the *individual;* it also talks of Moksha or salvation of an individual and not of a group or a community. There are quite a few modern Tibetans who lament over Tibet not having an army. Notwithstanding a strong belief and faith in non-violence in their personal and community lives, the new generation Tibetans feel that their country should not have been so weak militarily. Dalai Lama is not just a religious leader, he also is endowed with strong political sense. He is not at all orthodox or conservative like a religious leader; on the contrary, he is practical, with a correct vision for the future. His Holiness said in 1993, "I am certain that totalitarianism in China will go. There will be a more democratic atmosphere. Already more & more Chinese are showing sympathy and concern for the Tibetan nation, their culture & human rights; if they get more opportunity to express their genuine feelings, I am sure this problem can be solved easily. I am foreseeing that change towards freedom and human dignity."[40]

Chronology of Major Events

A.D. 605-650	Tibet an imperialist power. Invention of the script & propagation of Buddhism. (Mahayana).
750-800	Tibetans capture Sian (China's capital).
822	Sino —Tibet treaty.
850-1100	Break-up of monarchy, rise of feudalism & monastic authorities.
1270-1368	Mongol (Yuan) dynasty rule over China & Tibet.
1368	Mongol dynasty overthrown.
	Han (Ming) dynasty established.
	Tibet—China relations broken.
1642-82	Dalai Lama becomes the undisputed sovereign of Tibet.
1652	Dalai Lama visits the Manchu emperor.
	Dalai Lama's help sought to contain the Mongols.
1720	Manchu authority over Tibet.

1850	End of Manchu suzerainty (over Tibet).
1912	End of Manchu dynasty.
	Tibet & Mongolia declare independence.
1951	17- Point Agreement between People's Republic of China and Tibetan Autonomous Region (led by the Dalai Lama).

Sino-Indian Relations

All students of history in India have to compulsorily go through the immense contributions of the Chinese travelers like Huen-tsang and Fa-hien to the early stage of written (Indian) history; we are also told, with great pride, about Ashoka the Great's able son and daughter, Mahendra and Shanghamitra, who "spread" the message of Lord Buddha to East & South-east Asia, including China. This period can be called the beginning of relations between China and India though, in those days these civilizations were not political units; even territorially they were loosely knit. The relations were neither good nor bad, since the kings, feudal chiefs or the warlords in these countries were busy fighting with each other and grabbing each others' territorial expanse. They could not think or see beyond their immediate or encircling kingdoms; how could they be bothered about kingdoms or civilizations so far away?

Besides, Buddhism was quite a powerful bond. Common people had nice feelings about the neighbouring civilization mainly because of the appreciative accounts of these travelers,etc.; both the civilisations nurtured a sense of awe towards each other. The relations remained cordial due to an unspoken sense of camaraderie against British imperialism. Both were finding it difficult to combat. Relations did not become sour, not even after the British attempts at creating breaches by drawing artificial lines of political boundaries like the notoriously disputed McMohan Line. Both the nations, including Tibet (whose political position was like that of a buffer) were suspicious of and unhappy with Great Britain because of its imperialist motives. Independent India had hailed the People's revolution in China. It aimed at having friendly and co-operative relations not only with China but also with all other neighbours—big or small. The famous Bandung conference of the "non-aligned" and the newly-independent nations (1955) was clearly indicative of this positively interactive atmosphere. Its outcome was the "Panchasheela" or the five guiding principles of international relations.

India had felt apprehensive of China's political motives and international stance in 1951, because of the latter's occupation of Tibet. She started feeling quite threatened since 1959 when the dispossessed Tibetan ruler, His Holiness the Dalai Lama, entered India ,followed by hundreds of Tibetans as refugees. The Defence "thinktank" of our country started expressing doubts about the British-drawn boundaries between the two countries. This culminated in the border skirmishes of 1962. PRC insisted that Chinese sovereignty over Tibet had been recognised for a long time by U.K., U.S.A. and U.S.S.R., and that the issue came essentially within its national jurisdiction. The PRC representative at U.N.O. questioned this body's right to bring Tibet within its agenda; he also warned that U.N. will be guilty of unwarranted intervention in the internal affairs of PRC.[41]

Jawaharlal Nehru, the Prime Minister of India at that time, had said "we are anxious that Tibet should maintain the autonomy it has had for the last 40 years. We do not challenge or deny the suzerainty of China over Tibet.....From whom are they going to liberate Tibet is not really clear to us!.....However, it is ,ultimately, the wishes of the people of this country that should prevail and not any legal or constitutional argument."[42]....The wind started blowing hot and cold between in the first few years after the continuous influx of Tibetans as refugees into India and particularly, over India granting proper political asylum to them. Over the decades things slowly and imperceptively got settled down, and India and China became good neighbours again. [It is really unfortunate that BJP xenophobia created a monster out of a friend in 1998 with the nuclear experiment at Pokharan!]

Indo-Tibet Relations

As mentioned earlier, for centuries Tibet felt closer to the ancient civilization of India, mainly because (1) Buddhism traveled from India and (2) there is no history of aggression or undue interference from India. It was believed that the first mortal rulers of Tibet had migrated from India. Ateesha Deepankara, revered as a mine of knowledge and spirituality, had also traveled from India. Buddhism had traveled to China also,but it could not have that radical and lasting influence on the thoughts, beliefs and socio-political pattern as it did in Tibet. [It will have to be a different study for the purposes of understanding the reasons behind that.] In Tibet the tenets and the principles upholding the utmost sanctity of life and environment (that conserves life) could flow and percolate into the society so smoothly, Buddhism, as the popular stories about King Ashoka and his son Mahendra and daughter Sanghamitra go, was transported to China, Japan, Sri Lanka and almost all over South and South-East Asia, but it stayed effectively and meaningfully only in Tibet & Sri Lanka. It brought gender-equality to the Sri-Lankan society even though geographically, culturally and historically it is so close to the Indian tradition of rigid divisions of the society and human-beings on the basis of gender and work /occupation. Buddhism strengthened the already existing norms and beliefs in the Tibetan society. Sanctity of life, environment and peace—in other words, non-violence, is the basic tenet of Buddhism and also the Tibetan society. Other societies of South, East and South-east Asia, which had embraced Buddhism, could not transcend to this height....could not get rid of the evils of their pre-Buddhist society. It is , thus, very important to enlighten ourselves with Buddhism, rather, Mahayana Buddhism, in order to understand why (1) the Tibetans remained so united, exclusivist and freedom-loving , (2) they are so cool and fearless inspite of having no army worth its name, and, most important by, why (3) they emotionally remain attached to their religion and religious leader—come what may.

Short History of The Tibet Region When Buddhism Entered

After the nomadic movements of the 2nd. century B.C., Central Asia had a peaceful existence which was not broken until the next wave of nomads from the east, beginning in the 4th. century. It was the beginning of another chapter when the Huns reached Europe and their cousins followed the invasion route to India (to the south). A different history got created when the city-states of the Tarim basin submitted to Han expansion. The rule of Wang Ming in China, in the very first years of A.D., had instigated revolts amongst these city-states and the Chinese tributary system could not get re-activated until the latter part of this dynasty. A famous General, Ban Chao, had secured allegiance to China from all the Tarim-basin states; but after the General's death,in 102 A.D., they regained their confidence to regain their independence. The influence of China was replaced by that of the Kushans.

Two very significant developments which changed or re-wrote history, were (1) the Indian merchants brought the Kharosthi and, later, the Brahmi alphabets—the mother of Tibetan & Bengali scripts. Many others in and around the same region were also based on these scripts. Secondly, Buddhism got actively promoted under the Kushans, spread by the monks in the Tarim basin. The same merchants traveled east to China also; but there is no clear evidence of Buddhism getting promoted alongwith. Trade with China continued and grew all the same and silk continued to flow to the European nations. These region were steadily and surely growing into mercantile, industrial and imperialist powers—much to the dismay of China.

The break-up of the Han empire did not directly lead to the rise of new powerful states. A chaotic political vacuum followed for almost a century; a few of China's subordinate allies claimed the legacy of the Han and declared themselves lords of northern China. At the same time, a good number of invasions took place from the North and there were strifes—often bloody— for hegemony or political superiority. The Xiongnu were followed by pro-Tibetan Qin dynasty (357-385 A.D.) and later by the Wei dynasty .The rule of the Toubo dynasty (after which Tibet gets its name) came to limelight between 398-577/581 A.D.

The Central Asian oases became veritable crossroads of western Asiatic, Indian and Chinese civilisations; these distinguished themselves from the oases culture of Russia and western Turkestan with regard to their languages, scripts, religions and fine arts. Chinese rule was badly disrupted by a series of revolts in many of the oases-settlements; the Chinese were even forced to withdraw garrisons from many remote and not easily defensible positions....Tang China maintained its rule till the end of the 8th. century, mainly against Tibet, which gained power in Xinjiang during 670-692, and again in 790-866.

Kroraina was an important station on both the silk routes (the northern as well as southern).Its agrarian output was never large enough to feed the local population; its livestock production (donkeys, horses, camels) was an important source of support for the mercantile activities. Buddhism is first traceable in this region in the 2nd.century B.C. We know of text fragments in Syriac, Middle & New Persian, Mongolian, Tibetan, Chinese, etc.,written in twelve different kinds of scripts. Major texts belonged to the religious sphere—more precisely to the three world religions of that time,viz: Buddhism, Nestorian Christianity and Manichaeism.[43]

Precepts of Buddhism as Practiced in Tibet

In order to understand why and how religion played and continues to play the most important socio-psychic role in the Tibetan society, we must, briefly go into the essence and the basic tenets of Mahayana Buddhism. In this context, the ten meritorious acts (dasapunnakiriyani) should be taken into consideration. They are

(1) dana (donation or generosity)

(2) sila (honesty or morality)

(3) bhavana (thinking or concentration)

(4) patti (transference of merit)

(5) pattanumodana (rejoicing in receiving merits)

(6) veyyavacca (rendering service to those whom it is due)

(7) apacayana (reverence to the deserving)

(8) desana (instructive preaching)

(9) suti (listening to instructive preaching)

(10) ditthiju (correction of views.)[44]

Society has a far more important place in the life of a Tibetan....An individual lives for and works for his /her society or community; the importance of an individual lies solely in the fact that without him/her there can be no community and no society can be formed. That is why no.6, viz: rendering service to those whom it is due, along with nos.9 & 10, viz: listening to instructive preaching and correction of views mould and guide their lives. This is the basis of lamaism ; this also explains strength of their character ,marked by an admirable attitude of tolerance, contentment and love for peace & non-violence. The queer importance of the institution of Dalai Lama in their life and society gets amply explained by the dominance of these principles in their lives. They not only believe that "listening to instructive preaching" endows them with "merit", but they also believe that receiving merits is a matter of great "rejoicing". Of course, "paying reverence to the deserving" is the most obviously observed characteristic of this community. Instructive preaching refers to a wider and more comprehensive range of activity, covering the entire social-ethical behaviour of the individual.

The Four Behavioural Patterns of Kindliness (Catu Sangaha Vatthu) are of equal importance in this context. They are Dana, Piya Vacana (use of pleasant words in communication with others), Atthacariya (resorting to beneficent actions) and Samanattata (equality). These principles or guidelines of behaviour attempt to show the right path to the Theravada Buddhists (the particular sect prevalent in Tibet specially) to bring about harmony and concord among the members of the society. Buddhism, in advocating these modes of behaviour, has highlighted the reciprocity in rendering services....How a society can benefit from the practice of Parmitas (perfections) is also of immense significance. Both Mahayana and Theravada speak of the value of attaining ultimate Perfection.[45]

It may not be wrong to say that any religion has a twofold duty to perform, viz: (1) delineate the moral path of life based on its world-view, and (2) emphasise the value of reaching the supernatural & transcendental goal (for real & permanent happiness) conceived in terms of its world-view. Durkheim, a pioneer in the field of Sociology, explained how cohesion (in a society) is maintained by religion. Quite a few other Sociologists felt the same and elaborated a fourfold social role of any "working" religion. They are:-

1. Maintenance of social solidarity,
2. Providing answers to the problems of life,
3. values & norms for the society, and
4. psychological /moral support to its followers.

And this is exactly what religion has done for the people of Tibet; that is why the sacred words are like the guiding star in the life of a Tibetan. Social and moral (religious) life of a Tibetan., therefore, is intermingled and inseparable.

The Words of My Perfect Teacher by Patrul Rinpoche is not a treatise for experts but a manual for anyone sincerely wishing to practice Dharma. The unique literary style was eminently suitable not only for the illiterate nomads and villagers but also for the lamas (highly educated in theology only, otherwise illiterate). This book—quite similar in style and content to the famous Geeta of the Hindus—is ,perhaps the best-loved introduction to the foundations of Tibetan Buddhism and is, therefore, highly recommended by the Dalai Lama and other eminent teachers. It opens our eyes to the enormous value of human life, particularly to the seminal dictum of Ateesha Deepankar, the great traveler-messenger from the original land of Buddhism. Almost all the research and writings on Tibetan Buddhism have been inspired by the curiosities & inquiries about Ateesha, and volumes have been written on his unfathomed knowledge and contribution....The dictum is "the best spiritual friend...is the one who attacks your hidden faults." In addition, a vast number of teachings introduced into Tibet from India (from 8th. cent. onwards) and countless commentaries on all the three "vehicles",viz: Vajrayana, Mahayana & Shravakayana, written by Tibetan masters, exist. This lineage got passed on, unbroken, from one realized teacher to the next, until the present day. Albert Einstein, once pointed out that Buddhism fulfilled the criteria necessary for a spiritual path adapted to the 20th. century.

A human life can be called "precious" human life only when it is complete with all aspects of freedom & advantages. Without freedom there is no "precious human life", however extensive one's knowledge, learning and talent (in ordinary things) may be. Freedoms and advantages do not come by chance or coincidence; they are the results of the accumulation of merit & wisdom, built up over almost one's lifetime.[46]

> To find this precious human life
>
> Is more valuable than finding a precious jewel...
>
> To see the real nature of mind
>
> Is more valuable than meeting the Buddha.

All the wealth of the world would still not give you the power to take as much as a needle and thread.[47]

There are people who, because of their past actions (Karma),become the subjects of an alien ruler or the slaves of a rich person and ,thus, lose their freedom completely. Rinpoche Longchenpa said,

> You would like to keep this excellent human life with its
>
> freedoms and advantages
>
> Forever, but you are certain to die.
>
> You would like to study Dharma with your wonderful teacher

Forever, but you are certain to part.

From today put on the armour of effort,

For the time has come

To cross to the land of great bliss whence there is no separation.[48]

"The Words of My Perfect Teacher" goes on to warn the followers thus— "to have wrong views—even for an instant, is to break all your vows and to cut yourself off from the Buddhist community. It also negates the freedom in this human existence to practice the Dharma. From the moment your mind is defiled by false views, even the good you do no longer leads to liberation...."[49]

Khu, Ngok and Drom, three main disciples of Ateesha, got enlightened by the following belief—

The best quality is a great desire to benefit others.

The best accomplishment is a steady lessening of negative emotions.

The best discipline is a peaceful mind.

The best wisdom is not to grasp at anything at all.

Wisdom is the self-liberation from grasping and clinging....

It is free from false convictions, it is beyond "samsara",

It is supreme peace.[50]

Discussion on Tibetan Buddhism or the Tibetan's anchorage to Dhamma will remain incomplete without explaining how deeply ingrained is the idea of Karma in the life, actions and beliefs of an average Tibetan. (It is an equally significant belief with the Hindus.) They firmly believe that they had to leave their beloved land and become refugees because of nothing else but their Karma, and therefore, they should consciously desist from bad deeds and go on striving to become better and better. They forget a very crucial part of their spiritual guides' teachings i.e. Karma, or the inevitable effects of one's good or bad actions through rewards and punishments (or good or bad lives in future) is necessarily individual and never experienced collectively. Each individual is wholly and solely responsible for his /her actions as for the bliss or curse, accordingly. We need to deal with that, in some detail, in the next chapter.

References

1. H.E. Richardson, *Tibet & its History*. (OUP, New York) 1992.
2. Charles Bell, *Tibet: Past and Present* (OUP, London) 1924.
3. *op. cit.* 1.
4. *op. cit.* 2.
5. Kunzang Lama I Shelung, *The Words of My Perfect - Teacher*, (translated originally by Patrul Reupoche). (Harper Collins Publishers, India). 1996.
6. *op. cit.* 2.
7. David Snellgrove & Hugh Richardson, *A Cultural History of Tibet* (Weidenfield & Nicolson, London) 1968.
8. *op. cit.* 2.
9. *op. cit.* 1.
10. Nirmal Chandra Sinha, *Considerations on Inner Asian History* (Firma K.L. Mukhopadhyay, Calcutta), 1967.
11. Wang Gia-Wei & Nyima Gyaincain, *The Historical Status of China's Tibet* (China Intercontinental Press), 1997.
12. *Ibid.*
13. A. Tom Gruinfeld, *The Making of Modern Tibet*, (OUP, Delhi), 1987.

14. *op. cit.* 11.
15. *op. cit.* 10. The Chinese are once again trying to prove their suzerainty in the affairs of the Tibetan by declaring Karmapa as the real spiritual head, as apposed to Dalai Lama. PRC is also trying to establish that what the Mongals had done was not correct.
16. Graham Sandherg, *The Tibet and the Tibetans.*
17. *op. cit.* 10.
18. *op. cit.* 11.
19. *op. cit.* 11.
20. *op. cit.* 7.
21. *op. cit.* 11.
22. *op. cit.* 1.
23. *op. cit.* 11.
24. *op. cit.* 13.
25. *op. cit.* 13.
26. *op. cit.* 13.
27. Ram Gopal, "*India - China -Tibet Triangle*" (Pustak Kendra, Lucknow), 1964.

27a. In the mid-19th. century, a kingdom of Western Tibet invited the famous Indian scholar Ateesha. He established Buddhism in Tibet and is specially known for having formulated the Tibetan lunar calendar with 60 "year cycles".

28. Michael Van Walt Van Praag, *The Status of Tibet* (Wisdom Publications, London) 1987.
29. Charan Shandilya, *Tibet on March* (press copy of the manuscript), Delhi, 1998.
30. *Dalai Lama, Tibet, China & the World* (a compilation of interviews, Narthang Publications, Dharamshala, H.P. 1989. & Dawa Norbu, *Red Star Over Tibet.*

31. *Tibetan Women: Oppression and Discrimination in Occupied Tibet* (National Report on Tibetan Women issued by the Tibet. Ad. in Dharamshala for the Fourth World Conf. on Women, Beijing), 1995.
32. *Dalai Lama—My Land and My People* (Asia Publishing House) 1962.
33. *Ibid.*
34. *op. cit.* 29.
35. *op. cit.* 31.— Quatation marks show the biases and beliefs of those who fled; these may not be realities.
36. *op. cit.* 30.
37. *op. cit.* 29
38. *op. cit.* 32.
39. *op. cit.* 11, 29.
40. *op. cit.* 32.
41. Shen Tsung-lien & hiu Shen-chi, *Tibet & the Tibetans* (Stanford University Press), California, 1953.
42. *op. cit.* 27.
43. *op. cit.* 10.
44. Ananda K. Coomaraswamy & I.B. Harner, *The Living Thoughts of Gotama, the Buddha* (London, 1948).
45. G.B. Upreti, *Early Buddhist World Outlook in Historical Perspective.* (Calcutta, 1998).
46. *op. cit.* 5.
47. *op. cit.* 5.
48. *op. cit.* 5.
49. *op. cit.* 5.
50. *op. cit.* 44.

2

Introduction to Tibet and The Tibetan Society

Tibet has always been a land of great fascination, mystery and romance. It has always captured man's imagination and is rightly called the 'Hidden Kingdom in the Heart of South-Central Asia', 'Jewel in the Lotus', 'A Distant Horizon', 'The Land of Snows', 'The Roof of World', 'A Lost World', Shangrila and by many other superlatives. This land of fascination remained inexplicably secluded for centuries. Though recently it has opened its doors to the outsiders, all the glamours arising from its sublime serenity have remained unaffected and a full and accurate account about the Tibetan people and their ways of life has still not been available.

According to a rough census taken in 1982, the population of Tibet is 1.89 million of which nearly 51.4 percent are females and 48.6 percent males. This means that there is no tampe ring with demography unlike in India or China.The population in Lhasa, which is the largest town of Tibet, is roughly 35,000-40,000. It rises to 70,000-80,000 during the Great Prayer Festival. The second largest town of Tibct is Shigatse which has a population of 13,000-20,000.

The third largest town is Chamdo in eastern Tibet with a population of 9,000 to 12,000. The fourth largest town is Gyantse in central Tibet. Its population is about 8,000. Besides there are many smaller towns and villages. Out of the total population of about 100,000 Tibetans, who have left Tibet, about 50 percent are women[1]— a fact which indicates that there is no gender bias against Tibetan women.

Chinese travelers of the 8th century spoke of Tibet as the Kingdom of Women. Arthur Waley has also mentioned in his book 'Western Pilgrimage' that in Tibet women ruled over men and men were subordinate to them. The 33rd King of Tibet, Songtsen Gampo who is held in high esteem by the Tibetans, greatly honoured women. Buddhism is the religion of Tibet and in it the status and role of women are not only high but also very respectful. Songtsen Gampo adopted Buddhism and then married two Buddhist wives.

Women have always been very active and hardworking. In the rural areas, women did most of the work related to agriculture. Some write that Tibetan men are less laborious and active. It is also written that all sins were ascribed to women when carnality was considered a sin and celibacy holiness. According to a rough estimate, 1/5 of the male population lived in monasteries. Women's role in pastoral and agricultural areas was dominant.

Women in Tibet enjoy an equal and respectable status, and never had to observe purdah or the veil system. They wield influence in home life and business and control family accounts. But, Tibetan men do not indulge in the hypocrisy of 'Ladies First' and 'Fair Sex'.

In Tibet there are no 'outcastes' since according to Buddhism, everybody is equal in caste. Based on occupational work, Tibetan society could be divided into monks and nuns, noblemen, merchants and traders, farmers, nomads, etc. The status of women vary accordingly. Owing to their significant role in agriculture and animal husbandry very few women adopt a religious life. Among the nobility were families who rendered service to the Government or to the Dalai Lama. A "noble" woman leads a life of luxury being dressed in costly costumes and adorned with precious and semi-precious stones studded in ornaments.

A Tibetan is a born trader. Large monasteries also carried out trade and noblemen were also traders.

Farmers and ranchers were the common people of Tibet, and they lived in the river valleys, especially in the southern and south-eastern parts. Some farmers were tenants of the government or the monasteries and land was sometime given to them in return of taxes and labour services. Some were hired or drafted labourers. Only a few farmers owned land. It is difficult to imagine the immensity of the labour they had to put forth in the fields or in the construction of houses and monasteries. Women who worked as labourers were clad in rough cloth and tunic, fully powdered with dust. They worked in full faith, for the construction and renovation of the monasteries in Tibet. They had only one set of clothes and could not take bath for several months.

Nomads, called Drok-pa, were mainly herdsmen and shepherds. They grazed their animals on the steppes at higher altitudes which are not suited for agriculture. They were very hard-working and sturdy. There were semi-nomads who adopted a settled livelihood for part of the year and were nomadic for the remaining time. Women of the labourers, the farmers and the nomadic class were full of stress and strain.Their duties were considered to be limited to home, that is, maintaining the household. But running business and helping in agriculture and livestock were also important duties.

In pre-1959 era, there was almost no participation of

women in administration or state affairs. Women were treated in a different way in all matters including their upbringing and education. Several respondents replied that discrimination among women (under feudalism) cannot be ruled out. In Tibet a large number of population belonged to the ordinary middle class or to the lower class and the status and life of women varied according to the differences in the status of their men in the society.

Tibetans followed an exogamous rule of marriage, that is, a member of a clan was not permitted to marry within his clan upto 7th generation. Cousins in the eighth generation onwards were allowed to marry among themselves.

In addition to the system mentioned above, the Tibetans followed the norm of class endogamy. Aristocrats married within themselves as it had a political impact. In case of some exceptions or dissolution of marriage the sanction of the government was required. Three types of marriages were in vogue viz.,

1) Monogamy
2) Polyandry and
3) Polygamy

Any form of marriage was acceptable so long as it did not involve division or disintegration of the family property. Most people were and are monogamous. This view is mentioned by scholars like Heinrich Harrer (1956) and corroborated by Swami Pranavananda (1960). Wealthy or high ranking officials, noblemen & landlords usually kept several concubines besides their own wives. Polygamy was considered a symbol of social status.

Thus, in a nutshell, there were 4 kinds of households in Tibet:

1. One in which several men kept several wives.

2. One in which several men kept only one wife.
3. One in which one man kept several wives; and
4. One in which one man kept only one wife.[2]

Polyandry was common among the poor, where several brothers shared one wife and worked together to support the family. This practice is common in India in some of the areas bordering Tibet. Sometimes in a poor family several sisters shared one husband. Sometimes mother and daughter shared the same husband. In such a case, the mother usually married a husband younger in age to support the family and the daughter married the step-father if she was already "mature" or later, when she reached marriageable age.

Polyandry is closely connected with the principle of keeping the property in one hand. The property which the ancestor have left behind to the posterity should not be allowed to disintegrate. This is evident from the fact that if a brother leaves the paternal house & settles down elsewhere independently with a wife of his own without accepting his brothers' right over her, he would forfeit the right to the property of the family.

There are several cases of polyandry or plurality of husbands in Tibet. These cases are: (1) when several brothers share the same woman as their wife, (2) when two or more men, not brothers, marry a woman by mutual agreement, (3) when a married woman gains influence over her husband and with his consent marries another in addition. In all these cases, the woman exercises her authority over her husband.[3]

Usually both the bride and the groom are of the same age except in some rare cases. Generally the parents arrange the marriage except in a few rare cases when the girl selects her husband. In arranged marriages the parents may not even take the consent of their daughter.

In Tibetan society widow marriage is common. A

widow not only can remarry, in fact it is considered essential for her and her childrens sustenance, protection and security. A very interesting example has been given by a famous Tibetologist Dawa Norbu (1974) citing the example of his own family. He said, his mother remarried as she wanted "to have a strong partner who could saddle, load donkeys and continue petty trade. In short, she remarried for the care and the future of her children. A father-less family has to remain in great stress and strain." Sociologists opine that widow marriage is very logical, taking into consideration the kind of life in Tibet. There is no stigma on the life of a woman even if she remarries several times. There is no difference in respect and prestige which a step-father commands in the family and he is treated equally like a real father. This is also required for economic reasons.[4]

Divorce is not so common in Tibet owing to the value attached to the stability of relationship in a Tibetan family. In the case of a divorce, the woman's right is always well protected. When a wife with a son/sons is divorced she is entitled to one-fourth of the common property. If a divorced wife has a daughter she is entitled to one-sixth of the property. If she has no children she could claim an unspecified amount known as 'wages for day and night'. This was before the new democratic constitution of the Tibetan Government in Exile.

Generally divorces are discouraged. If any marital discord arises in the family then the relatives and friends try to settle it and bring about reconciliation between the husband and the wife. Divorce is considered very bad for the couple and for the reputation of the whole family. Tibetans consider that marriage is a life-long relationship.

In Tibet there was a great deal of freedom in man-woman relationship. Though married couples were very faithful, the unmarried, particularly the young people, often took the license of having pre-marital sex. Man and woman relationship is regarded to be natural. Sex is considered to be an important basic need.

In this regard, it is worth quoting some observations by Rahul Sankrityayan (1953), "At places where men and women were engaged in forced labour, I observed that during their work men and women exchanged jokes, sang and enjoyed themselves in joke and frolics." Some other Tibetologists have also mentioned that no one observed shyness or inhibition in matters of sex. Tibetan women are not prone to insolence and depression. They are always jolly, ingenuous and good-humoured.

Family planning in the modern sense of the term was not known to Tibetans before 1959. However, several intelligent children were initiated into monkhood which, in a way, resulted in reducing the size of a family; and that was the reason why for several years the population of Tibetans remained constant. The institution of polyandry, especially among the agricultural and pastoral people was responsible for limiting the birth rate and thus to keep the population stationary. It is also responsible for a comparatively higher standard of life though the land is poor and not very productive.

Rahul Sankrityayan (1953), a famous Indian Tibetologist noted that most Tibetan women do not believe in family planning. They believe in providence and god's will. Those who are engaged in agricultural and pastoral life desire to have more children (like in all backward agricultural economies). The Tibetan women however feel that it is difficult to give birth to and bring up children in Tibet owing to the hard and busy life they have and also to the cold climatic conditions. But now, i.e. in exile, with the availability of certain facilities against difficult climatic conditions and due to living, as they do, a more sedentary life, Tibetan women have been reported to get pregnant even at the age of 50.

Fertility was low in Tibet, but among the Tibetans in exile the fertility rate has gone up.[5]

It is believed by Tibetans that a woman, though she may be charming and good-looking, should first reincarnate as a man before she can attain Buddhahood. From this angle women in Tibet are inferior to men in status. But this belief has no impact on their practical life.[6]

Religion is very important for Tibetans. Though there were disparities in the socio-economic status, there was almost no discontentment. This may be due to the fact that the religious aura, which enveloped the life of the Tibetan people, made inequalities appear natural, normal and non-injurious. Religious impact is very powerful and women, like in most societies, are more religious-minded than men. In the changed condition in exile, inspite of an attitude towards materialism, religious fervour is still foremost in their minds. There is a private chapel in every house of a Tibetan, rich or poor. Even in a tent there is a small corner set apart for worship. In the shrine there are images of Buddha, and other saints made of gold or silver. In front of the shrine butter lamps burn day and night and bowls of water in small vessels are arranged in rows. In the households, best fruits and delicacies are offered to deities before the family members eat. On waking up, elderly ladies say short prayers by lying face down in front of the shrine several times. At breakfast, after dipping the forefinger of her right hand into her tea she would raise and flick it three times, thus to offer to three precious things of Buddhism, (the Buddha, the scriptures and the body of monks). In the evening the mother or the most elderly in the family rotates her prayer wheel and chants prayers for everybody to listen while, at the same time, turning her rosary. Just before going to bed, she says a short prayer. Religious rites and ceremonies are performed in the monasteries. The smell of incenses, flickers of butter lamps and chanting of men, women and monks pervade the monasteries. Sometimes, on special days, fasting is also observed. Old Tibetan women strongly believe in the concept of 'Heaven' and the theory of Karma. They are always very hardworking and never sit idle.

Kalachakra (Dukhor Wangchen) sermons are delivered by the Dalai Lama. The present,i.e. the 14th Dalai Lama, performed one in Leh (Ladakh) in 1976 and in Bodhagaya in 1986. There was a large congregation which was equally attended by women. The Tibetan women, on the whole, are holding traditional threads and weaving the fabric of religio-social life in the new set-up.

Religion is a very important factor in Tibet and anything which is against religion is bound to meet with hatred and resistance from the society. Practice of religion gives more and more confidence to overcome one's weakness, get enlightenment and be free from rebirth.

Buddhism totally rejects the theory of social stratification based on caste and speaks of the unity and the oneness of humankind. Caste system originated on the basis of race prejudice originating in the minds of the early Aryans who invaded North India. The migrant Aryan invaders had to deal with a kind of people different in appearance and having a totally different culture. These original inhabitants of India were named 'dasyu' and introduced as 'dark skinned' (Kala varnah), 'noseless' (anasah), 'revilers of Vedic gods' (deva piyu), 'devoid of Vedic rituals' (akarman) 'non-worshipers of Vedic gods' (adevayu), 'non-sacrificers' (ayajvan), 'phallus worshipers' (sisna devah), 'non-adherers to Vedic practices' (avrata), 'lacking in devotion' (abrahman) and 'followers of a different religious ordinance' (anyavrata).

The Vedic hymn continues: "We are surrounded on all sides by dasyu tribes. They do not perform sacrifices.

They do not believe in anything. They are not men. O Destroyer of Foes! Kill them.[7]

Caste is not merely a religious dictum or a social custom; it is the reflection of a powerful /overpowering belief, ever since Man invented agriculture, settled down and, therefore, started becoming (i) conscious of his labour or productive efforts and (ii) possessive of the land and its produce. It is a belief that the human race is broadly divided into the strong & the weak, more competent & less capable and the owner & the owned. The owner and the powerful, naturally, would like to retain and maintain his power & property....in fact, human civilization could not have taken shape and gone ahead if not for this indomitable human urge for more & better. In order to retain and stabilise their power and authority they invented caste—a full-proof structure to divide the society, *permanently* and *through generations*, into the "haves" & "have-nots". The Aryans or the Vedic society in India made this division look natural and unavoidable by giving it a religious sanction. Caste- system, that is why, looks specially deplorable in the modern context of democracy and secularism.

But no human society is free of this malady (whatever name it may take). Feudalism, capitalism, apartheid, theocracy and patriarchy—all are different expressions of social divisions dictated by power & property. Pre-1951 Tibetan. society was no exception. A very detrimental type of feudalism-cum-theocracy ruled over there and the overwhelming majority of the people lived in rather sub-human socio-economic conditions. They, too, were victims of the denials of social,economic, educational and political opportunities as well as of religious freedom, justice & equality before law. The one and the only reason why Peoples' Republic of China extended its power and influence over Tibet, it claims, was to "liberate" its people from the evil clutches of feudalism.

(And, whatever its methods or approach, it has actually effected many a much-needed reform.)

B

Budhha, "the truly wise", appeared in India with his message of true egalitarianism, when caste discriminations and atrocities were reigning supreme. He preached, "if anyone (whichever caste he may belong to) kills creatures, takes what has not been given, wrongly enjoys the pleasures of the senses, is a liar, of slanderous speech, a gossip, covetous, malevolent in mind and of wrong views, he is destined to be re-born in a state of woe. But one who lives up to the standard laid down in the Dhamma—be he a Brahman or a Kshatriya or a Vaishya or even a Shudra—is a virtuous person and is destined to be re-born in a heavenly world.[8] Thus Buddhism, in no uncertain terms, speaks of the unity of mankind over and above racial, tribal & caste distinctions; Buddha's path of "realisation" was for one and for all—ignoring and denying any division or differentiation between man & man and man & woman. Buddhism, and many centuries later, Sikhism, were the only religions that gave almost equal rights and status to the so-called "weaker" sex and we notice its reflections in the Tibetan and Sinhala societies. (Sikhs, in practice, got very badly influenced by the highly patriarchal Hindu Aryan society around).

As mentioned earlier, Karma or the effects or the consequences of one's deeds or activities in this birth, to be suffered or enjoyed in the successive births, is as important a guideline for the Tibetans as it is for the Hindus. My observation of the Tibetan psyche tells me that the theory and fear of Karma is more overpowering in their day-to-day life than in that of the ordinary god-fearing Hindus. Almost each and every migrant feels, or is quite convinced, that they had to run away from their home-land because of their "collective" bad Karma and if they lead "virtuous" life here (away from home) they will be "rewarded" with their beloved motherland back to them. Within the compulsions of the present highly competitive and highly commercialised economy, combined with their State-less position, they try to remain as honest and religious as possible; and they try to compensate their failures by donating a significant amount of their income regularly to the monasteries. They abide by, strictly and blindly, to what His Holiness says or ordains. The overall result is extremely beneficial for the society, particularly for women. While copying democracy from the Indian political system the Tibetan government-in-exile became truly democratic and egalitarian....For Indians but, these values & ideals have remained a mirage. Forty-eight years of our "Democratic", "Secular" and "Socialist" Constitution has not made an iota of difference in the lives of women or any other discriminated & deprived group; on the contrary, there has been an increase in dowry-deaths, rape and other sexual & sexist violations. These evils have almost got institutionalised! [We shall learn about the details of this socio-political "revolution" in the migrant Tibetan society in the appropriate chapter.]

For Tibetans, Karma is closer to "the state of the system". Some human systems need more power, others need to be cooled off. Some systems need more compassion, others need increased input of intellectual wisdom. This is born not just from intellect, but from accurately sensing the flow and connection of events. Thus, with proper inspection of one's Karma, one neither abandons oneself to its flow, nor ignores it; one puts energy into directing it towards more productive ends.[9] Tibetan religion, in fact, is a complex intermingling of Buddhism (its Tantric form imported from India in 700 A.D.) with the even more ancient "Shamanism" of north-east Asia—a faith, according to some, of the North American Indians.[10] It places primary emphasis upon maintaining harmony in the realms of both outer & inner experiences. Teachings are oriented towards establishing a harmony of mental events.

C

Feudalism—the ownership of the land and the labour

As pointed out right in the beginning of this chapter, the traditional Tibetan society was divided into two major classes—aristocrats & serfs. The landed property was shared by Gum-ba (the monastery) & Ku-dra (nobility & the officials in charge of political administration). The latter had both official and private holdings. Of the three types of estatés, viz: government, religious and private, the total tax from the lands, except those owned by the monasteries, went to the government. At least one male from a "noble" family served the Dalai Lama and the son-in-law did in the event of a noble not having a son.

On the basis of socio-economic and ritual factors, we can classify the traditional Tibetan society as follows:

Division I: Priestly Class - The Lamas

(a) The high born wealthy or learned monks,

(b) The lower clergy-illiterate ones.

Division II: Nobility

(a) Descendants of early kings,

(b) Descendants of the Dalai Lamas' kin,

(c) Descendants of those who are ennobled for their services to the country.

Division III:

Descendants of yogins, meditators and nature

controllers, or the descendants of the Senior Lama (N gak-pa) in whose case marriage is legally allowed.

Division IV:

Rich people-Lords and officials (Jinda or Ge-ri-kh and Ger-pa).

Division V:

Common men (Pha-lba or Me-mong)

1st Stage: (a) Peasant (Shing-ba)

(b) Nomad, (Drok-pa)

(c) Trader (Chong-ba)

2nd Stage: (a) Idol (mud) worker, (Jim-so-wa)

(b) Stone cutter (Do-so-wa)

(c) Potter (Zan-khem-ba)

(d) Tailor (Chem-so-wa)

Division VI: Craftsmen

1st stage: (a) Goldsmith (ser-so-Che-mo-la)

(b) Silversmith (Ngu-su Che-mo-la)

2nd Stage: (a) Coppersmith (Sang-so-wa)

(b) Blacksmith (Ghar-Shan)

Division VII: Lower Castes

1st Stage: (a) Fisherman (Nya-pa)

(b) Hunter (Ling-ba)

(c) Ship builder (leather) (ko-ba)

2nd Stage: (a) Descendants of ex-prisoners (Ku-ma)

(b) Beggar (Pango/gy awa)

Division VIII: Outcastes.

(a) Butcher (Shem-ba)

(b) Corpse dispatcher (Tam-den)[11]

The land-holding pattern indicated a man's status & power in the society; a woman's social status was according to her "patriarch's"—as it is in any other patriarchal society. A feudal society, necessarily, has to be patriarchal. Power originates and thrives on division. Therefore, any power-structure has to support all divisions and injustices. We shall see how all gender-inequalities got automatically evaporated with the firm establishment of democracy in their polity in exile. On the other hand, this gender equality is also an indicator of true democracy. All forms of equalities and equities are complementary, and gender equality is the most fundamental of all equalities and equities.

This Tibetan variety of class-division was slightly less offensive than the Indian type of class division, viz: caste-system, because the former offered a scope of coming out of one's social position and not remain irrevocably bound by birth; anybody, for example, could enter the nobility by becoming a government servant. The father and brothers of the Dalai Lamas and all the close relatives automatically entered the nobility though, in reality, nobility by deed, and not solely by birth, was almost non-existent. One knows what a vicious cycle socio-economic backwardness is. So even if the "space" was allowed or offered, a serf or a lowly born could hardly ever "come up" to occupy that space. A change can be effected by a powerful people's awareness to the magnitude of a revolution (as it was as a result of communist movements in China, Russia, etc.) or by a genuine pro-people move by the government (as we see in the case of the Tibetan government-in-exile).

One silver lining to the cloud was that there were unbound serfs also. They were free to work for whoever they found suitable. But, they had to, *all the same*, work for somebody or other. They could never earn enough—inspite of bargaining options— to buy or own land. Inadequate income , along with permanent dependence on other's land, got them bound invisibly. Bound labour, like in India, was bonded through generations—the daughter had to work for her mother's lord and the son for his father's.

Another important reason why the Tibetans, except the monks and the members of the nobility, remained perennially backward was the absence of any opportunity for education. And this is what they are happiest about in exile. For the first time in the history of Tibetan civilization the Tibetans, of all ranks & categories, got full opportunities for education in both Tibetan Autonomous Region and India. Women, too, got equal chances. The education provided by the Central School for Tibetans is welcome to the privileged /educated class also (the class which was allowed to get educated in the traditional society) because the traditional or ecclesiastical learning was of no use and cannot be of any use in the modern, highly competitive world. The only purpose that education used to serve in pre-1951 Tibet was to give them the high status in the society. It was quite a common practice, among them, to send their children (girls also) for modern /Western education to various English-medium schools in the Darjeeling district of West Bengal in India. It is on record that almost all the female relatives of Dalai Lama got educated in the prestigious Christian missionary schools here.

We have discussed above that only the lamas & the nobles had the right /privilege to education. This kind of social discrimination was quite similar to the system during the Vedic days, when only the Brahmans & the Kshatriyas were privileged and powerful and could get trained in "Shaastras" & "Shastras", i.e. religious scriptures and the art of weaponry.

D

That status of privilege obviously, the ex-nobles could no longer enjoy in the changed circumstances. Therefore, it may not be too wrong to believe that

1) it was these dispossessed groups that organised the "great escape". They found themselves most vulnerable in the face of anti-feudal measures from PRC; to lose wealth, status & power all together was a little too difficult to accept. A certain section, though not very big in number, strongly believe that if Tibet had been ruled by the British, for example, it would have been free "easily" like India. They, obviously, are fully unaware of our people's fate during the centuries of British oppression and tortures. They think that Britain and America, or the industrialised countries from the West, are not so "uncivilised" like the communists, who take away from the 'nobles' what is "due" to the "people" and destroy people's culture in the name of destroying feudalism, etc.,etc. Besides, they also believed that the British believe in democracy, etc., etc.

They had definitely managed to bring some wealth with them; they enjoy a better standard of living and own relatively posh shops and restaurants,etc. They are English-speaking and command the confidence and style of an aristocrat or a well-placed government official. They, (perhaps), manage to get along better with the equally snobbish Indians or tourist-customers. They do not have a language/

communication difficulty. But, definitely, they do not command higher respect or awe from the less-educated or the less prosperous Tibetans.

It is important to note here that there was a trend / tendency to elect /select such English-speaking, *confident* women as President or Secretary of Women's Associations because (a) liaison with non-Tibetans or English-understanding Indians was important and necessary and (b) the "uneducated" Tibetan women, belonging, originally, to a lower socio-economic rung, did not wield the required confidence and smartness. But, now the women elect only really committed and hardworking women. They are good at talking to, arguing with and can convince Tibetan men and women of all categories and occupations. Therefore, competence in Tibetan language is more important though preference is for those who are also comfortable with English and /or local Indian language.

2) It was, also, in their vested interest that the deposed nobility wayled the innocent, ignorant, ready-to-believe common people by propagating that the pro-people reforms, like modern education, modern health facilities, modern communication methods, factories & industries,etc. were mere "hoodwinks" and that freedom of the country (i.e. its territory) was much more important and necessary than the type of individual freedoms the Chinese are 'appearing to offer'.

3) This section of the society had everything to lose & nothing to gain from the "populist" measures imposed by China. With loss of status and the possible "oppression" of "equality" the new system could bring, the best possible option left to them was to become anonymous i,e, start afresh in a totally new environment /society. They therefore, took the maximum initiative in organising Dalai

> Lama's flight. That predictably, created a panic and gave a rationale to their propaganda against the Chinese "aggression". Their flight to neighbouring, non-communist and "friendly" India looked rather justified. The equality "imposed" by their own government-in-exile does not really affect them, since in the changed circumstances there is no class-division and all the migrants—to whichever class he may have belonged to in his traditional society—have taken up jobs /profession to suit his convenience or capability.

E

Equality & The New Set-Up

The new landholding pattern has, naturally, brought considerable change in the refugee's social life and thinking. They are provided with *equal* amount of land on *individual* basis. Everybody is a landowner during his /her lifetime and the land has to be returned to the Settlement Corporation after the owner's death; it cannot be inherited by the children automatically. ...Education too, is now available to each and every migrant and is compulsory. The class-differences are now unknown and thoroughly mixed up, So, even the doors of monasteries are now open to everyone.

The Tibetan women's love for freedom must have been very powerful, lying dormant for centuries due to an extremely unequal socio-economic structure. That is why it was not difficult for them to assert when the shackles were removed. (It does not happen in our society. Even a highly educated, economically independent Indian woman does not necessarily assert or start enjoying freedom). The men also found it sensible and expedient to acknowledge equal rights for women when the Constitution of their new democratic government had granted that and their religio-temporal head,

His Holiness the Dalai Lama, had endorsed. It was in their interest to remain strongly united in an alien atmosphere. Strong unity was possible only in an atmosphere of equality and true freedom.

References

1. "*The Tibetan Population: Past, Present & Future* (New Star Publishers (Beijing, 1994).
2. A.V. Arakeri, *Tibetans in India: The Uprooted People and Their Cultural Transplantation* (Reliance Publishing House, New Delhi, 1998).
3. I.B. Harner, *Women Under Primitive Buddhism* (Motilal Banarasidas, Delhi. 1975).
4. Dawa Norbu — *Red Star Over Tibet.*
5. *Life in Exile* (Central Tibetan Relief Committe, Dept. of Home, Dharamshala, H.P., 1992).
6. op. cit. 3.
7. A.C. Bouquet, *Sacred Books of the World* (Cassel, London, 1962).
8. Ananda K. Coomaraswamy & I.B. Harner, *The Living Thoughts of Gotama, the Buddha* (London, 1948).
9. Peter Gold, *Tibetan Reflections: Life in Tibetan Refugee Community* (Wisdom Publications, London), 1984.
10. *Ibid.*
11. Tieh-Tseng Li, *Tibet: Today and Yesterday* (NewYork), 1960.

3

Basic Tenets of Buddhism, Tibetan Buddhism & Lamaism

A

It is important and necessary to acquaint ourselves with the basic tenets and philosophy of Buddhism and,with the "way of life", prescribed by Lamaism; this kind of background will facilitate our understanding of the Tibetan society, Tibetan mind, their way of thinking and way of life. They are:—

A. Suffering (Duhkha). This is regarded as the First noble truth or truth of the nobles (meaning those who have noble virtues in them). The awareness and the experience of this makes one conscious of the (i) source of suffering, (ii) cessation of suffering and (iii) path (marga) leading to "dharma".Each noble truth has three aspects. The first is characterised by (a) misery of suffering, (b) misery of change (because all pleasures are temporary and inevitably followed by pain) and (c) misery of motivations (because "karma" inevitably is followed by "klesha" or suffering).[1]

The typical prayer-wheel of the Tibetans has sets of

12 turnings symbolically representing 4 truths:3 aspects.

The miseries,e.g.,are birth, old age, sickness, guarding one's valuables, not possessing valuables,etc. And, to dispel pain of hunger there is food, to dispel pains of heat, cold and shame there are clothes, for sleepiness beds,for commuting vehicles and for illness there are medicines.

B. Karma, the second noble truth. The notion is quite similar to the Hindu belief of Karma. Karma, however long-lasting, can ultimately come to an end. "As to the maturation in this life the fruit of Karma matures. At the time "Siddhi"(success) is attained, (the evil effects of) Karma are warded off and cause and effects are then abandoned....Life, then, becomes like the sky."(translated from Tibetan).

During 38 weeks of pregnancy "winds of Karma" are claimed to influence foetal progression.

C. Seed Consciouseness, the third noble truth. Thought of enlightenment is like father-seed and insight intuiting non-self is like mother-womb. The act of creating seeds is a characteristic faculty of human consciousness.[2]

Though the source of origin of life, viz: the seed, is the father (quite similar to the Hindu belief of the "male" as the creator), from the mother the child derives "all essential substances", i.e. all the physical and mental characteristics & features. Mother enjoys a very special position of honour and reverence in Tibetan. thinking; mother's love is glorified as "boundless love and boundless compassion" and she is regarded as the Parent No. 1.But it is widely and genuinely believed that the mother cannot protect or rescue, only father can. That is why, widowhood is discouraged, widow though not despised. (Unlike in the Manu-shastra or Hindu rituals, widows do not face discrimination, disgrace or torture).

D. Dharma, the fourth noble truth. It leads one to the path to the end of suffering. Three instructions need to be followed, viz:

(i) morality (adhishila)

(ii) mind-training (adhichitta)

(iii) insight (adhipragna)

Dharma,thus, guides and regulates our Karma and is, therefore, "good in the beginning, good in the middle and good in the end....a continuum."[3]

The theory of Karma also gives a lot of importance to the "death experience". Since rebirth is inevitable,"death consciousness","death vision" and "death-time act" to determine next life are of equal importance."The Munis do not wash away defilements (of the stream of consciousness) with water (as though it were a matter of washing away dirt);do not remove suffering with hand (as though it were a matter of pulling out a thorn).....they liberate the beings from the cyclical flow by the teaching of the truth of real nature (i.e. absolute truth); the beings got to meditate on its meanings." [Tibetan annotational commentary].

The next vital belief of the Tibetan is in *Virtues* or *Perfections*. Bodhisattva's firat perfection is in *Giving*. Whether or not there is concrete/actual giving, what is important is the volition of giving. In Tibetan philosophy, therefore, there is no conception of "more" or "property".

The second perfection is of *Striving*, the *third* of *Insight* and the *fourth* of Common Pursuits.[4] The stress is on the word "common"; unlike in the Hindu theology, there is no discrimination /distinction of high or low, superior or inferior.

Man is composed of six elements, viz: earth, water, fire and wind...plus...space(akasha) and perception or understanding (vijnana).[5] "One cannot become enlightened through a contrived mind. Rather, the basic mind is to be identified, in relation to which all phenomena are to be understood as the sport of the mind".[Dalai Lama,Nov.23,1990]. Patrul Rinpoche, in his "The Words of My Perfect Teacher",says "there is nothing so uniform as water, nothing so creative as the wind, nothing so far-flung or elevated as error and nothing so correct as the measuring rod"—a rather interesting way of reminding us of the hard realities.

The next important concept is of the *Teacher*. Teaching is the "great vehicle" and time is the ever-revolving wheel of eternity.The teacher embodies the essence of all Buddhas He is the union of three Jewels—his body is like Sangha, his speech is like Dharma and his mind is like Buddha. The Teacher tells,

> I've shown you methods
>
> That lead to liberation,
>
> But, you should know
>
> That liberation depends upon yourself.

Unless you practice Dharma according to Dharma, Dharma itself can become the cause of evil (rebirths). This is the most fascinatingly eye-opening guidance from a guru (teacher)! (How I wish the religious bigots of all other civilisations understood this !) This explains why the Tibetans have an unquestioning trust in and obedience to their religio-temporal leader Dalai Lama's wisdom and also why they honestly endeavour to do what have been explained to them as good and virtuous, including their superbly democratic Constitution given to them by their government-in-exile.

> "Bless me and foolish beings like me
>
> That we may attain the very essence of

The freedoms and advantages,"

The teacher truly means it and the pupil strives best to keep upto this prayer or the "blessings" he /she receives.

The next significant feature of Tibetan/Vajrayana Buddhism, that strengthens the Tibetan. mind further, is their deep belief in *Impermanence.*

> Impermanence of the outer universe in which *Beings* live
>
> Impermanence of the beings, living in the universe
>
> Impermanence even, of the Holy Beings, i.e. so many Buddhas, and, specially,
>
> Impermanence of those in positions of power.

This is where this religion is so pragmatic and egalitarian. In contradiction, Hinduism and most other religions talk of absolute power and clear-cut power-hierarchies. Emphasis on the theory of impermanence is laid thus:-

> Causes of death are numerous,
>
> Causes of life are few
>
> And even those may become causes of death.

The Buddha said,"to meditate persistently on impermanence is to make offerings to all Buddhas, and to be guided, inspired and blessed by them."[6]

The following are the "wrong doings", which causes suffering, re-birth and further suffering—

(1) Taking life,i.e. (a) killing out of hatred

(b) killing out of desire,e.g. animals

(c) killing without knowing if it is right or wrong. The most condemnable killing is of father, mother and a teacher; even creating schism within Sangha is considered bad a crime.

(2) Taking what is not given—by force,by trickery or stealthily. Business or commercial activities are looked down upon because these involve "piling up" and "corruption".

This explains why Tibetans, in general, are quiet, soft-spoken, amiable and peace-loving. Though they are successful traders and shopkeepers, they are generally honest with their customers and do not aim at lots of money or a very high profit—which is possible only by hook or by crook. They like good living, but feel ashamed to get marked out as rich and different from others. There are no forced divisions on the basis of occupation (which used to be in pre-1951 feudal Tibet), class or gender. They believe that greed leads to property, property to corruption, and these together lead to power. Power can survive only on division, hatred and oppression. But these cannot happen if people are devoted followers of the Teachers and their teachings.

(3) Sexual misconduct

(4) Lying

(5) Sowing discord—particularly among members of Sangha.

(6) Harsh speech

(7) Worthless chatter

(8) Covetousness

(9) Wishing harm to others

(10) Wrong views,i.e. to think that Buddha's words, Teacher's instructions or the texts of the learned commentators are in error or to doubt and criticise them.

The severest of the sins are "taking life" and holding "wrong views".[7] The Buddha said—

> The joys and sorrows of beings
> All come from their actions."
>
> "Do not take lightly small misdeeds
> Believing they can do no harm;
> Even a tiny spark of fire
> Can set alight a mountain of hay."
>
> "Do not take lightly small good deeds
> For drops of water one by one
> In time can fill a giant pot."
>
> "When the moment comes to leave, O King,
> Neither possessions, friends nor family can follow;
> But wherever beings come from, wherever they go to
> Their actions follow them like their own shadow."[8]

The next important advice to the people is about arousing *Bodhichitta* or training the mind for Four Boundless Qualities, viz:

(i) boundless love

(ii) boundless compassion

(iii) boundless sympathetic joy

(iv) boundless impartiality.[9]

The last quality is regarded as the most important and binding, because love, compassion or joy tend to be one-sided and, therefore, not pure. It is, also, advised that the best method to arouse compassion within oneself is to imagine *Oneself* to be the tormented person. and true impartiality is achieved when one is able to give up hatred of foes and infatuation for friends. This height of noble mentality (which appears rather unattainable) can be reached when one is not only able to put oneself in others' position, but also consider others more important than oneself. All these are results of true *Wisdom*, which can be attained through (a) hearing, (b) reflection and (c) meditation. Merit and wisdom are regarded as two rich "accumulations" and one needs four *Powers* to accumulate. They are—

(i) power of support (from teacher, teachings, one's faith, understanding, determination,etc.). It is through faith that absolute *Truth* can be realised.

(ii) power of regret (for negative actions)

(iii) power of resolution (against negative actions and for positive actions)

(iv) power of action (i.e.positive action as an antidote to negative actions).[10]

Patrul Rinpoche says—

Being born in the hell, in the "preta" realm,

As an animal, long-lived god or a barbarian,

Having wrong views, being born when there is no Buddha,

Or, being born deaf or mute

These are the eight states *without Freedom*.[11]

Pretas are the body-less spirits; but in this context they are the evil spirits. The long-lived gods have no opportunity to practice Dharma, because they spend their time in a state of mental blankness. (This notion is quite similar to the beliefs of the Vaishnavs and the mystics in India.) Those, who lived in the 32 border countries or outside the "cultural" realm of Tibet or where there was no Buddha, have been referred to as barbarians. The word does not bear the degrading connotation of the Western imperialist civilization.[12]

A human life can be called a "precious human life" only when it is complete with all aspects of freedom; however extensive one's knowledge, learning or talent may be, one does not have a precious human life without freedom.

> To find this precious human life
>
> Is more valuable than finding a precious jewel
>
> To meet a perfect teacher
>
> Is more valuable than gaining a kingdom
>
> To see the real nature of mind
>
> Is more valuable than meeting the Buddha.

Freedoms and advantages do not come by chance or coincidence; they are the results of an accumulation of merit and wisdom.[13]

'*The Words of my Perfect Teacher*', by Patrul Rinpoche ("Rinpoche"means wise or learned or teacher or all combined), is constantly recommended by the Dalai Lama and other eminent teachers as a manual of practical advice for anyone sincerely wishing to practice Dharma. It was written in a style that could convey as easily to the nomads and the villagers as to the lamas and the monks. The writer was a firm believer in Ateesha Deepankara's dictum that the "best spiritual friend is the one who attacks your hidden faults." Ateesha was the first monk and a wise man to travel to Tibet from India and is still revered as one of the five most venerated wise men. Khu, Ngok and Drom, the three main disciples of Ateesha, were told that

> The best scholar is one who has realised the meaning of *no-self*
>
> The best monk is one who has tamed his own mind
>
> The best quality is a great desire to benefit others

> The best remedy is to know that nothing has any inherent reality
>
> The best accomplishment is a steady lessening of negative emotions
>
> The best sign is a steady decrease of desires
>
> The best wisdom is not to grasp at anything at all.

Another Teacher, Rigdzin Jigme Lingpa, said,

> Wisdom is the self-liberation of grasping and clinging
>
> In it there is neither thinking nor a thinker.
>
> It is free from false convictions.[14]

Albert Einstein had, once remarked that Buddhism is a tradition that could fulfil the demands for a spiritual path adapted to the 20th. century. Gender equality and genuine love for Nature and environment of this culture should become a model for the 21st.century. We in India, should strive to adopt that. It should not be difficult if we really want so. After all, these values are very much in our Constitution.

B

Tibetans say "government of the God, by the God and for the God," though, in reality, it is of the God, by the God and for the people. People of Lhasa refer to Dalai Lama as "Tse" meaning the peak (it is both figurative and locational). He is not supposed to have direct dealing with the people; the liaison officer is, therefore, called "Tse Ga",i.e.front of the peak. There are two important books of Law. The first contains 10 Commandments for the Holy Order and 16 Articles for the laity. The second book is composed of 13 Commandments from Gyan-ch'u Gye-tsen (14th. cent.).It is elaborate, covering everything from petty thefts to the conduct of a ruler.

Tibetan religion places primary emphasis upon maintaining harmony in both realms of outer and inner experiences. Political ideologies advocate peace from without, i.e.world peace through economic readjustments, equitable distribution of wealth and, ultimately, a classless society. But, can that bring stable and permanent peace unless man's craving impulse becomes and remains controlled. Inner reform has to be effected i.e. peace has to be established from "within", viz: in the mind. Right mode of thinking, therefore, is the best method /approach to peace. Principle of non-violence is the basic concept upon which the ideal of peace is founded. Non-violence exists only in a mind which is totally free of craving, greed, lust and a sense of superiority (ego). And, wealth is not an end in itself: it is only a means to fulfill social and religious obligations. There is need for two accumulations only—*Merit & Wisdom.*[15]

All human beings are born free and equal in dignity and rights. They are endowed with reason and conscience and should act, with one another, in a spirit of brotherhood. One, who is deprived of inner peace, will not be able to propagate peace in society. If man is to survive on this earth, peace has to be sustained. Peace is an art of survival without which we cannot speak of happiness on this Earth, nor of human rights and values, nor of the achievements of human civilisations. Buddhism, preaching the unity of mankind, unfolds a way of life for the betterment of the quality of life here and hereafter. But, this rich, remarkable socio-ethical aspect of Buddhism, particularly of Tibetan Buddhism, has not been adequately emphasised.

Tibetans are taught, from infancy, to be mindful of their own actions, especially of those that affect others. Systematic and conscious endeavours towards the "purging" of harmful or unbeneficial thoughts—not just the avoidance of such acts—is a very important and necessary exercise.

New Year is marked by symbolic purgings of such thoughts and feelings. They effectively turn their energies towards building a better /ethical year. One notices an indescribable energy that emanate from these devout people when they are near Dalai Lama or have a glimpse of him. There is a dramatic exhilaration of body and soul /spirit. They believe that Dalai Lama will remain for ever as long as he is kept away from "inordinate negative" influences and feels able to work *for* and *on behalf of* his people and all other sentient beings.[16]

The Tibetans believe that in order to practice true Dharma one must,first, seek an authentic spiritual friend—a teacher who has all the necessary qualifications. Then, one should obey his instructions, praying to him from the depth of one's heart and considering him real Buddha. It is only through faith that absolute truth is realised. Unlike "Upanishadas" or any typical Hindu scripture, Buddhist literature is not that of "Notes" of a "School",but that of sermons, delivered to a number of persons—very often a large concourse. Repetitions are wearisome, but they enable the faithful to memorise and thus, remember better and effectively.[17] Another significant reason why this religion or faith is so humanistic or people-oriented is that there is no general theory of "revelation" (unlike the Vedas or the Holy Quoran): the Tripitaka or the Jataka are "naturalistic human records."

> I lay no wood, Brahmin, for fires on altars;
>
> Only within burneh the fire I kindle.

The way one listens to Dharma is very important, but even more important is the *Motivation* with which one listens to it. "Unless you practice Dharma according to Dharma, Dharma, itself, becomes the cause of evil...rebirth." (Dagpo Rinpoche).

C

Caste-system, or discrimination on the basis of parentage and occupation, imposed by the dominant, but minuscule minority called the Brahmins, over a vast section of the majority, was a reigning feature of the Aryan /Vedic civilization and Buddhism was the first of the many movements that came up as a strong resistance. That is why, naturally, Buddhism preached and propagated an ethical way of life—guidelines for thought and action of all people (without any categorisation). Buddha raises a crucial point. "Brahmin women also have periods, conceive, give birth and breast-feed like a Shudra or any other woman....the colours of her breast-milk and blood are the same..."

None is, by birth, a Brahmin,
None is, by birth, an outcaste;
By deed one becomes a Brahmin,
By deed one becomes an outcaste.

"He who has completed the noble life and has reached the end of all passions—him I call a Brahmin." Many centuries later, Shri Chaitanya a mystic saint from Bengal, has said exactly the same thing.

Such an egalitarian "ism", prescribing such an egalitarian way of life, was, unfortunately, not all that egalitarian about the position and the role of women. Motherhood was the most important responsibility and role of women; they received highest reverence and care as a mother. The other roles were as daughter, wife, widow and woman worker. It is important to note here that it was only in this society that a woman's role as a worker or, in other words, a woman's contribution to the productive process, has been recognised. No other religion, no other way of life, not even liberal democracy, has ever recognised the special role of the dominated sex as an agent of production.

But, like in all other religions of the world, the woman was suspected and accused of low sexual morals and seducing the man. (After all, all Gods, Prophets and preachers are necessarily male.) There has been a long dialogue between Buddha and his very close disciple Ananda where the former is against women becoming nuns and the latter arguing in favour. Buddha said "women-folk are uncontrolled, envious, greedy and weak in wisdom...and, therefore, danger to monks...and the attainment of pure life."... "Waves, alligators, whirlpools and dolphins are the four dangers to religious life; and women are like dolphins."

Defeated, ultimately, by Ananda's logic,persuasion and perseverance, Buddha granted the right of nunhood to women, but put 8 discouragingly stringent conditions. Women happily accepted. Defeated, Buddha said, "if women had not gone out of household life to enter a homeless state, pure religion would last long...good laws would stand fast for 1000 years..." It was also propagated that only a man can attain enlightenment. Under Mahayana Buddhism but, a queen took a vow that she would be born again and again and yet attain enlightenment.....She did and has been deified as goddess Green Tara." Tara is particularly revered and worshipped by the Tibetan Buddhists. This shows how the seed of "equal respect for women" was sown in ancient Tibetan thought.[18]

In Kapilavastu, a daughter of the Sakyas,named Gopika, abandoned woman's thought and cultivated man's thoughts and was, therefore, reborn as a son. This is a very good example of the Buddhist theory of Karma emphasizing the belief that the mind eventually determines the body.

Some of the gender-discriminative duties imposed on the nuns were:-

— a bhikshuni, even if senior, has to rise and pay

obeisance to a bhikshu;

- a nun cannot admonish a monk, but a monk can admonish a nun for real or unreal offences;
- penance & seeking instructions every half month and ceremony of repentance is a must for a nun after every rainy season.

And, as a strategy, the marriageable age for girls was being continuously lowered thus ensuring less and less possibility for women to become nuns.

However "rebellious" this religion may have been, after all it was born in an Aryan mind and in the land of the Aryans whose only aim was absolute power and absolute power can be ensured and maintained only by the institutionalisation of division and discrimination that creates absolute fear. And fear about the opposite sex, which,in no way, is inferior or less capable is the most overpowering fear in the minds of those who hanker after power. So even if Buddha could think of complete equality among men, he could not conceive of a perfect equality with women. Yet, what he preached and believed in was far ahead of his time and a formidable challenge to Manu and the prevailing socio-economic structure. There was no place for oppression and exploitation of women in the socio-religious system he conceived and propagated. Girl-child was equally acceptable to a married couple. Buddha had told King Prosenadi of Kosala that "a girl may prove a better offspring." Monogamy was strictly advocated. The husband was ordained to give respect, courtesy, faithfulness, adornments and,even authority to the wife and the wife's duties were hospitality to the kin of both sides, faithfulness, watching over goods husband brings and skill & industry in discharging all her "business" (duties). Widow could inherit her late husband's property. Texts are silent on her re-marriage.

Though a category of women-workers has been recognised in the Buddhist society, they,like in all other societies under patriarchal religions, were not allowed or expected to be productive. Women in rich or well-to-do households were expected to do household work only, since their men-folk were bringing home enough to support the family. But, women from poor families were allowed to be in self-supporting trade and agriculture.

But, Tibetan feudalism, like any other feudalism or, in other words, stagnant economic system, did not implement this woman-friendly part of the Buddhist doctrine. Women as acrobats, musicians, courtesans from this economically disadvantaged class were socially accepted though, majority of them earned as domestic workers in the wealthy households.

There were three major classes in the Buddhist society, viz: agriculturists, wealthy merchants and the slaves, even if Buddhism was committedly against caste and slave systems. Buddha ordained that the work allotted to the servants should be according to their physical strength and the master must be humane and reasonable. The slave should have the right to equitable wages and full meal, with occasional delicacies. He/she should also be entitled to leave and medical benefits. And, the servant /slave should be honest, active and punctual.[19] Labour rights, won by arduous & lengthy trade unionism after the Industrial Revolution in Europe, it seems, have been proclaimed by Buddha two and a half millenniums ago.

D

The elements that make up the society are manifold. Husband & wife, taken together, are considered to be the most fundamental social unit having reciprocal relations. Likewise, parents & children, teachers & pupils, friends & companions, laity & priesthood, employers & employees form other social units. Every social unit necessarily requires bilateral commitments of reciprocal interest. At the same time, without individuals a society does not exist. Hence, the *individual* must be conscious of the duties that he has to perform for the smooth functioning of social relations. Keeping these criteria in mind, the individuals have been grouped into 6 categories according to 6 directions, viz:

East : Parents /Children

South: Teachers /Pupils

West: Wives /Husbands (interestingly, wives have been put before husbands and in all other categories the elderly and the more experienced have been placed first).

North: Friends /Companions

Zenith: Clergy /Laity (as expected, highest importance is given to Dharma and the monks—by placing them on the zenith).

Nadir: Employers /Employees.

The reciprocal duties of each unit have been discussed,at length, in the Sigalovada Sutta.

A child towards parents—once supported by them, it should, now, be support for them and it will transfer merit in due time. (It is compulsory for the adult children, whatever the sex, to take care of their aged parents, grandparents. It is a law even in non-Buddhist Communist China.)

Parents towards children—restrain them from vice and exhort them to virtue; also, hand over their inheritance in due time.

Pupils towards teachers—eagerness to learn and attentive learning.

Teachers Towards Pupils—training them well and making them masters of what they have already learnt. The teacher should also praise them to their friends & companions.

A husband towards his wife and a wife towards her husband as well as employers towards employees and employees towards employers— duties of mutual fulfillment of goals, i.e. complementary duties towards each other and towards the society.

Laity twards community of monks—treating them with affection in act, speech and mind, keeping one's house open to them and supplying them with their temporal needs.

Community of monks to the laity—restraining them from evil, exhorting them to do good and loving them with kindly thoughts, revealing to them a way to a heavenly state.[20]

Individual health of each unit contributes to the society as a whole; welfare of the individual and of the society are closely interdependent.

E

Buddhism came to Tibet in the 7th. & 8th. centuries and got smoothly and peacefully amalgamated with the existing Bon religion. This successful blending, as Lobsang Lhalungpa says, was a strong indication of Buddhism's ability to adapt beautifully to the local conditions while retaining its innate doctrinal purity. For example, the Tibetan symbols of four elements,viz: tiger, lion, eagle and dragon, are used in Tibetan Buddhism. Prayer flags on the roof-tops,etc. also indicate the continuation of Bon practices incorporated in Tibetan Buddhism. This religion is also unique in having embraced the essentials of both Theravada and *Mahayana* Buddhism. *Vajrayana*, typically Tibetan, contains Tantric belief and practice of India, but is based on the Mahayana concept of Nirvana. Buddhism received active encouragement from king Khri-Srong-Idebstan (late 8th. cent.) when the Tantric master Padmasambhava was invited from India. There was a debate, around the same period, to decide if the Indian or the Chinese form of Buddhism should be adopted in Tibet. Needless to add, the Indian side was the winner. Ateesha Deepankara, the Mahayana master from Bengal (India),gave a profound impetus to Buddhism in Tibet and he is, ever since, placed in the rank of the Five Great Religious Masters[21]—a position and honour much above that of Dalai Lama.

Dalai Lama does not seem to be wrong when he claims that Tibet has a long association with India and has been deeply and extensively influenced by Indian culture and religious thoughts. The Tibetans, he says, feels an emotional bond with the Indians and, therefore, India was their first and best choice to settle down when they had to leave their own land. Fortunately for them, their minds and their indigenous culture have worked as sieves; they have not been influenced by any negative aspect of the Hindu /Aryan civilisation. The Tibetan society has remained much less oppressive or unequal.

Saint Padmasambhava, a Rinpoche (guru) was the founder of *Lamaism* in Tibet. A lama also is a teacher who is well-versed in the doctrines of Dharma and well- equipped to guide his pupils in the path of Dharma. The 5 sacred books of this land, known as Shungchen Kapunga, are placed on the altar in each household and worshipped. But these are too tough for lay persons (however highly educated he/she may be); only Dalai Lama and a few highly learned lamas have the right kind of training to understand and explain. Ngaring Chemo is commonly read and understood; it, basically, guides people in the path of Nirvana by (i) Duwa (reading sacred books) and (ii) Ngo (meditation). It also guides them on rituals.

"Life-cycle rituals" is a rather unique and striking belief-cum-practice of Tibetan Buddhism. The idea behind is—all human beings have to pass through certain stages of their life prescribed by the society and at every stage of social recognition certain rituals got to be performed, because an individual does not become a member of the society, automatically, merely by being born. They are called Life-Cycle Rituals or Rites of Passage (as termed by Van Gennep)... For example, the "naming ceremony" initiates a new-born into his /her society; he /she enters into a new relationship with his family /community and is, simultaneously, entrusted with duties and responsibilities also. [We shall delve into the details of various such examples when we shall discuss, in details, the various customs and rituals related to women and their status in the society.]

Monasteries being the seats of religious activities. play important role in the lives of commoners, They attract modern, secular Tibetans also in times of festivals and celebrations. The believers come to pray and to offer food, money,etc. when their prayers are answered and their vows are fulfilled. Most of them regularly donate part of their incomes to the monasteries, believing that it will earn them merit (punya). It is also an ideal place for social get-together and exchanges—quite similar to the courtyard of the Hindu temples in the pre-medieval days.

In Tibet, monasteries or where the Lamas stayed, were exempted from paying taxes or service to the government. Yet, they had lands and serfs attached to them.

References

1. Kunzang Lama I Shelung, *The Words of My Perfect - Teacher*, (translated originally by Patrul Reupoche). (Harper Collins Publishers, India). 1996.

2. *op. cit.*1.

3. *op. cit.*1.

4. *op. cit.*1.
5. G.B. Upreti, *Early Buddhist World Outlook in Historical Perspective.* (Calcutta, 1998).
6. Ven. Pategama Gnanarama, *An Approach to Buddhist Social Philosophy* (Ti- Sarana Buddhist Association, Singapore), 1996.
7. *op. cit.*5.
8. Ananda K. Coomaraswamy & I.B. Harner, *The Living Thoughts of Gotama, the Buddha* (London, 1948).
9. *op. cit.* 5.
10. *op. cit.* 6.
11. Kunzang Lama I Shelung, *The Words of My Perfect - Teacher*, (translated originally by Patrul Reupoche). (Harper Collins Publishers, India). 1996..
12. Nirmal Chandra Sinha, *Considerations on Inner Asian History* (Firma K.L. Mukhopadhyay, Calcutta), 1967.
13. *op. cit.* 11.
14. *op. cit.* 12.
15. *Dalai Lama, Tibet, China & the World* (a compilation of interviews, Narthang Publications, Dharamshala, H.P. 1989. & Dawa Norbu, *Red Star Over Tibet.*
16. Peter Gold, *Tibetan Reflections: Life in Tibetan Refugee Community* (Wisdom Publications, London), 1984.
17. A.C. Bouquet, *Sacred Books of the World* (Cassel, London, 1962).
18. I.B. Harner, *Women Under Primitive Buddhism* (Motilal Banarasidas, Delhi. 1975).
19. *op. cit.* 6.
20. *op. cit.* 16.
21. *Ibid.*

4

The Unique Institution of The Dalai Lama

The Tibetan society is primarily a Buddhist society and there is a deep and continuing impact of Buddhist thought and code of instructions /guidelines even to this day (unlike in other Asian civilisations where Buddhism had originally spread). The impact of the institution of Dalai Lama is not only typical and unique to Tibetan Buddhism, but also a historical legacy that has to be properly understood in order to clearly understand the Tibetan society in all aspects and in all ages, including at present. The basis of this uniqueness is the deep, unshakable belief that 'the Dalai Lamas are the re-incarnations of the previous Dalai Lamas, who, actually, are the re-incarnations of Avalokiteshwara, the Bodhisattva of Compassion'. Let us hear in the words of the present Dalai Lama.

"Buddhists believe in the theory of re-birth. Those, who *can* choose the time and place of birth according to their wish, are called re-incarnations. Those, who have extra-ordinary compassion, are believed to be the re-incarnations of Avalokiteshwara, the Bodhisattva of compassion or the

Dalai Lamas. This does not,however, mean that all the Dalai Lamas have one continuous consciousness."....[1]

The present Dalai Lama is endowed with extremely modern and progressive thinking, totally unlike a spiritual leader in any other religion...He is a thorough democrat and much more gender-sensitive than the best of the secularist. He is pragmatic with an admirable world vision. He does not believe that he, himself, is a re-incarnation. He talks of four types of re-birth. The most common type is one who is totally unable to determine his /her re-birth. The opposite of this is a completely enlightened Buddha. The third (type), due to past spiritual attainments, can choose, or, at least influence, the place and situation of re-birth. The fourth is called a blessed manifestation, who is blessed beyond normal capacity to perform helpful functions, like teaching religion. He feels that he is not sure to which category he, himself, belongs to. At the same time, the present Dalai Lama is quite happy in the assigned role of Avalokiteshwara, because, through this role, he can be of "great benefit" to his people. He has a "Karmic relationship" with them. He, in fact, considers himself "lucky" because, this role enables him to "serve his people." Shantideva, in his treatise on Engaging in the Bodhisattva Deeds, said—"as long as space exists, and as long as there are migrators in cyclic existence, may I remain—removing their suffering."....

"I always consider myself a Buddhist monk first. I feel that is real me", says the present Dalai Lama. "As for the Dalai Lama as a temporal ruler, I feel the Dalai Lama is a man-made institution." The latter identity is for the people to accept and continue to accept, "but being a monk is something which belongs to me: no-one can change that....In my daily life, I spend 80% of my time on spiritual activities and , only 20% on Tibet, as a whole.....Regarding politics, have no modern education except for a little experience. This is something I am compelled to do because of my people's hope and trust....I may not participate in the government if we achieve our political goal....I have always been attracted to Gandhi's way. He remained the key figure in India's freedom struggle; but, after independence, he remained aloof from politics. That is the proper way."

The present Dalai Lama further, says—"whether the institution of Dalai Lama remains or not, depends entirely on the wishes of the Tibetan people. I made this clear in the late 1960s. At the moment, this institution is useful to the Tibetan people, Tibetan culture" and their struggle. When the situation changes, this may cease to exist as a need, as an impact and as an impetus. "The Chinese are trying to present Tibet as having no problem except the Dalai Lama, who wants to reimpose the old system to regain his power and position" as a temporal head. To dispel this myth and fear, the present Dalai Lama announced that he is the last Dalai Lama. In the Constitution of the Tibetan Govt.-in-exile (1963) there is no post of the Dalai Lama or something similar to it. The abolition of the temporal powers of the Dalai Lama has been recommended by a two-thirds majority vote in the Assembly. A Reform Committee, with this aim, had been set up in Tibet, itself, in 1951. "Actually,"says the Dalai Lama, "the world was rapidly changing, and we, Tibetans, remained foolishly backward, not seeing or taking any notice of the changes going on in the outside world."

When asked "who explained to you that you are the incarnation of the Dalai Lama XIII, did you understand what that means, and how did you know what all to do", the Dalai Lama did not have clear answers. He was too young and totally uneducated and untutored when he was put to the throne of Dalai Lama.

Let us, now, look into some of the significant views of the Dalai Lama on religion, philosophy and way of life.

"Buddhism," he says,"is a way of life...a synthesis of philosophy and conduct. If you can help other sentient beings, then help them. If you cannot do that, then at least refrain from harming them. Not from the fear of sin, but rather from a compassionate attitude. You are your own master, everything depends on yourself. There is no creator. Tibetan Buddhism has something to offer to the world. Besides, the systematic training programmes for developing compassion, love and patience, there are quite a number of fields where Tibetan Buddhism and science can work together. As a Buddhist I don't accept the creator. According to Buddhist philosophy, one's own mind is the creator. Tibetans believe that their race had come into being when one monkey and one ogress came together and had children. This shows some sort of compromise between Darwin's theory and the Buddhist scriptures".[2]

Being a true democrat and humanitarian (incarnation of Bodhisattva, the Compassionate), the Dalai Lama holds an open and rational view even about Communism. If we go into the depth of both the "isms", and if we can manage to have an open mind ourselves we shall discover, to our great delight and surprise, that the fundamentals of both the beliefs are similar. As the Tibetan leader puts it, "Marxism is concerned with the distribution of wealth. This idea is something very positive and noble. The idea of Marxism is something for the majority and a sacrifice for the minority, and I think this is right. In Buddhism, particularly Mahayana Buddhism, there is emphasis on love and compassion—love for others. The essential part of the message is that it is absolutely worthwhile to sacrifice one's life and to work for the benefit of another person. Another practical reason is that you can find a large number of people in Asia who are governed by Communist countries. Among them there are a number of people who still believe in Buddhism even though they suffer for it. So if you can find a close relation between these two it will be very useful for millions and millions of people living under Marxism. Another thing, as time goes by it becomes clear that Communism cannot solve everything. Also, Communism is based more on hatred than on compassion. As a result, the Communist countries have destroyed mutual trust and respect for human values. In these fields, the Buddhist idea of compassion, love and even the methods of Buddhism might be complementary to the Communist methods.

Under these circumstances, I think some sort of dialogue between Marxism and Buddhism, especially Mahayana Buddhism, will be very beneficial to many people of this region. Real Communism is not created by force but by voluntary force in helping people to become less selfish. Communism is supposed to be for the benefit of the masses and not the minority. In order to do that, you need tremendous will and determination on the basis of altruism. Not by gun. Therefore, in order to achieve true general socialist ideas, some Mahayana Buddhist teachings such as altruism should be taught through reasoning and not through force. I feel that Mahayana Buddhism can be one of the factors that can help to achieve good socialism".[3]

The Dalai Lama holds strikingly eye-opening and thought-provoking views on the role and true purpose of religion. This, perhaps, is the greatest benefit of a religion or spirituality which lays highest importance to the good of all sentient beings, all "creations", and not to an abstract notion called the "creator". Religion should be down-to-earth, a way of life, and not injunctions of "supernaturals" from above the earth. He says, "Since there is such a variety of human beings mainly in the sense of mental disposition, one religion cannot serve all and is not sufficient. Practically in every religious field and teaching, despite the fundamental differences in philosophy, there is emphasis on the importance of love, compassion, forgiveness and tolerance. These are common in every religion.

If you think in a deeper way, then you can understand the various different religious values and reasons why so many different philosophies exist. If you think on these lines, then upon seeing differences, instead of feeling more apart you may get a feeling of deeper respect. Each religion is a special thing. Under these circumstances, it is extremely important that various philosophies and experiences exist. Not only of the similarities, but also the fundamental differences should be clear. A true and sincere practitioner, no matter of what religion, teaches the basics of love, compassion and forgiveness. If you belong to the human family you must show these qualities in the society, especially in times of difficulties.

My belief is that world peace should come through mental peace, through inner peace. Without inner peace it is very difficult to achieve genuine world peace. It is important to pay more attention to those activities which are non-violent. They involve reason, respect for human life, human compassion and human understanding. In our case, violence will be suicidal. My suggestion or idea is that demonstrations without physical violence will be better. Through non-violence, it may take us more time, more patience and more determination and the achievement may be small, but it is real."

Not all the Tibetans-in-exile, passionately involved in their struggle for the "liberation" of their motherland, are all that happy about their spiritual leader's views. "On a few occasions, youths who are a little militant come and argue with me, but I remain stubborn. Then they start crying," laughs Dalai Lama. "They love the Dalai Lama, but the Dalai Lama does not agree with their viewpoint, so they finally end up crying."[4]

The Dalai Lama is endowed with the kind of pragmatism and farsight that are normally found and expected in "Mahatma"s or the great personalities. He says that he, probably, is the last Dalai Lama. He feels, perceives and understands that his people are changing and have changed immensely, and this change, definitely, has been for the better and for their own good. "The old Tibet was backward in its technological and economic systems. Nobody denies this. But the virulent activists deny this. They propagate that everything was good with old Tibet and everything is bad in Tibetan Autonomous Region under People's Republic of China. The Dalai Lama also felt that this "change" is slowly, but surely, eroding the foundations below the institution of Dalai Lama itself. So, wisely he is advocating the abolition of this institution.

The Dalai Lama refers to Tibet as "a separate country from China culturally, geographically and historically."..He does not say "politically" or administratively. He has been laying stress on autonomy only and talks never of sovereignty. His wisdom tells him that complete independence or status quo will not really be possible without treading on the path of violence. He knows fully well that Tibet is no match for China on the path of violence. It is, rather, way ahead on the difficult path of non-violence, peace and amity. And, that is where the peace-loving and progress-aspiring Tibetans score and can get world admiration and support. "Now things are changing and are becoming more humanized. If the Chinese use their human understanding, then a mutual understanding can develop. Then for mutual benefit, I think, we can develop some sort of compromise which will be mutually beneficial. Under these circumstances, we have to consider the basic Buddhist doctrine and the motivation and the result is important. If the motivation is proper, then the result will be good. It will benefit the majority. I am a monk who always tells people the importance of compassion, kindness and patience, I always follow my own belief no matter how much people insist on the other way. Genuine non-violence is something like an experiment on this planet. If we succeed, it gains new meaning. Also, non-violence through human understanding and human love is something very new and very unique. If this experiment succeeds, it can be applied to other problems of the world. As Tibetans, we have to realize this special kind of responsibility.

On the other hand, I think it will be worthwhile for the world community to realize this thing even if they don't have sympathy for the Tibetans. It is an experiment and a unique fight. Violence is not our strength. Our strength is truth, justice, reason and human understanding. If we Tibetans use this strength then I think we can talk with the Chinese. If not in this generation, then in the next."[5]

Such statements show his firm belief in the major principles of Buddhism and how genuine he is about what he says and what he preaches. Seldom we meet a monk or a statesman so sincere, so honest, and yet, so pragmatic! He said "the Chinese have already occupied Tibet and it is very difficult for them to leave. Therefore, under these circumstance, it would be worthwhile to think of some middle path. Theoretically, I think it would be possible. On many occasions, I have said that the human boundary is always changing. Under certain circumstances, I explained, that two nations can be combined under one nation. Under other circumstances, the same community can be divided. The essential factor is that the concerned people get the maximum benefit. So, theoretically, we Tibetans, who number six millions, may get more benefit if we join the thousand million Chinese, rather than become an independent country. It is possible.I am concerned about the real benefits for the people of Tibet."[6]

These observations and statements are of deep

significance and must be made special note of. Inspite of being, primarily, a monk, (as he keeps on reiterating on innumerable occasions) his political wisdom is amazingly sound and correct. Very correctly, he realises the futility of the demand and struggle for the complete independence of his land because PRC is too formidable a power. The world-body or the comity of nations will not go beyond extending moral support only. So, on various occasions, in various ways, in subtle and changing languages, he goes on explaining to his people that it is in their interest that they recognise and accept the reality and divert their attention, energy and endeavour to the betterment and modernisation of their society and their individual lives.

But, as a spiritual-cum-temporal (political) leader he has to take full cognition of another equally important reality,i.e. psyche of his people. He must pay due respect to their sentiments and emotions. They are his children and they look up to their leader the way people do to their God in a theist community. So, he *also* talks of complete freedom, giving a philosophical /moral reasoning behind it. He knows that his people are intelligent, they understand their own good and are given to the values of democracy and progress, in keeping with the modern developed world. He also knows that his people (even if they do not admit) are adequately aware of the backward and retrogressive socio-economic system that prevailed in pre-1951 Tibet. They were cocooned in their "religious bliss", totally shut from the ever-progressing world. They are, therefore, very happy with their Democratic Constitution and their "modern" life, with first ever opportunities for universal education with a scientific thrust and secular content. The struggle is goaded more by emotions and a pride in patriotism than by any rationality or pragmatic thinking. So, he tries to guide his people in the path where the goal may be realistic and attainable. He says, "to improve relations between the Tibetan and the Chinese people, the first requirement is the creation of trust. Fundamental human rights and democratic freedoms must be respected in Tibet. The Tibetan people must once again be free to develop culturally, intellectually, economically and spiritually, and to exercise basic democratic freedoms. The Tibetans and the Chinese are distinct people, each with their own country, history, culture, language and way of life. Differences among people must be recognized and respected. They need not, however, form obstacles to genuine co-operation where this is in the mutual benefit of both peoples. It is my sincere belief that if the concerned partners were to meet and discuss their future with an open mind and a sincere desire to find a satisfactory and just solution, a breakthrough could be achieved. We must all exert ourselves to be reasonable and wise, and to meet in a spirit of frankness and understanding".[7]

The Dalai Lama, unlike a religious leader, is practical and realistic. He accepts reality without any remorse, condemnation or preaching; he is truly a people's Man / leader.

He moves with the demands of Time and for the "good /needs" of his people. He feels that "the Tibetan people, especially the younger generations, have changed a great deal. In some cases, they are even like Westerners. It is a way of life. At the same time, they have kept their Tibetan identity quite strong." Until now it has been like that. After a few generations, I do not know what will happen. It is unfortunate that the true Tibetan culture is now available only outside Tibet and not inside Tibet."

But, according to eye-witnesses, neither the monasteries nor the monks got affected in the slightest, except (in the Chinese leaders' own admission) during the "cultural revolution" frenzy. All those got rebuilt, as properly as it was possible, under the TAR govt.'s supervision. Video-films made by apolitical Indians are eloquent proofs of that. The numbers of monks and nuns have gone down drastically no doubt, but that is because avenues for (i) modern education, (ii) training in latest technologies and (iii) jobs according to one's choice and capability have opened up widely. (iv) The options for choosing one's career and life-style are also vast. Who would like to opt for a life of "complete denial" if one is not compelled by family or social pressures? The majority in any society believe in religion no doubt, but they do not like to choose the path of self-denial by becoming monks or nuns or ascetics. In fact, after a generation, there may not be a single nun. I could not come across a single family (in exile) whose daughters have chosen a path other than the mundane. Their long-cherished ambition of leading a life of their choice can now be fulfilled under their own government in exile. These films also show Tibetans in Tibet in their own dresses, performing their dances and other cultural feats. Signboards and names of shops, etc. are clearly seen written in both Tibetan & Chinese languages and, at places, only in Tibetan. The young girls— late school or early college students— who keep moving between India & Tibet, either to learn English or to visit their relatives, also say the same thing. They are discreetly silent when they are categorically asked about the extent of Chinese oppression in Tibet. I have talked to so many such but could not succeed in extracting any worthwhile information about the actual situation in present Tibet. Would these girls go back to Tibet? Would not they prefer to stay back here in India if things there were all that bad as it is told by the refugees to the sympathisers of the Tibetan cause?

As an answer to a question, "do you believe you will return to Lhasa one day?", the Dalai Lama replied, "I believe so. I am not very concerned about my own return. I am more concerned about my own usefulness. The value of human life is and in serving other people in helping other people as much as you can; so therefore I am really concerned about my own usefulness. From that point of view, if the situation changed inside Tibet, I would be very glad to return. But as I feel I can be of more use outside Tibet, I prefer to stay outside."

This is a rather ambiguous answer. Does he consider himself more useful from "outside" because he knows too well that a spiritual leader has no role to play in a totally reformed modern society? Or, is it because he feels that, even as a temporal leader, he has no role to play since the "new" Tibet of his dreams is already existing there? Or, is it because the 'democratic' system of exile will be faithfully carried to Tibet, whenever they return? On being asked "what do you feel about you being re-incarnated in occupied Tibet?", the Dalai Lama says,"if the Tibetans need another Dalai Lama for more or less the same circumstances, his reincarnation will be for the Tibetan people and culture". So definitely, the reincarnation will appear in a free country, not in the Chinese hands. The reason that the next Dalai Lama should appear, is to help the Tibetan people and culture. Thus he desires to appear among Tibetans who have freedom. In 1963, after four years in exile, a draft Constitution for a future Tibet based on a democratic system, was instituted. The constitution clearly mentions that the power of the Dalai Lama can be removed by a two-thirds majority vote of the members of the Assembly. The Dalai Lama claims that even when they were in Tibet in 1951, they had already set up a reform committee and carried out some reforms. The most revolutionary statement made by Dalai Lama was "as long as the Tibetan people respect the Dalai Lama, the institution will remain and work. *The institution was not made by God nor the Chinese people, but by the Tibetan people.* So, as long as the Tibetan people find this institution useful, it will remain." How wonderfully he has brought in democracy in the anti-democratic concept of 'Dalai Lama':

We must mark the word "useful". It is a rather carefully and thoughtfully chosen word. It shows that the Dalai Lama has a correct vision about the modern world and about what all his people need in order to become modern and competitive with the rest of the world. His beliefs and statements (presented in this chapter) can, thus,work as a guide and a model for any religious society, needing and seeking *rational* change. The Constitution of the democratic government in exile and, more importantly, the honest implementation of the truly egalitarian & gender-srnsitive laws are also fit for emulation, (even though, the Tibetan Constitution is a copy of ours, viz:the Indian Constitution).

References

1. *Dalai Lama—My Land and My People* (Asia Publishing House) 1962.
2. *Ibid.*
3. *Ibid.*
4. *Ibid.*
5. *Dalai Lama, Tibet, China & the World* (a compilation of interviews, Narthang Publications, Dharamshala, H.P. 1989. & Dawa Norbu, *Red Star Over Tibet.*
6. *Ibid.*
7. *Ibid.*

5

Democratic Constitution of The Tibetan Government In Exile

A

The primary aim of this study,let me repeat, is to explore into and understand the *New* Tibetan society that has "flowered" in the *New* soil of a different polity and culture. It is so dramatically different from what it was in Tibet. Unlike the trend in most of the "modernised" societies, this difference is for better-for true modernity. In this context, it is important and necessary to make a detailed study of their Constitution. That has to be accompanied by a correct understanding of their socio-cultural psyche, almost completely influenced by their religion and the overpowering personality of His Holiness the Dalai Lama.

The Constitution is quite a copy of the Indian Constitution or any other Constitution of the democratic world, where the principles of human rights constitute the foundation. Therefore, nothing new about it. But, what is new and striking is that, unlike with the majority of such Constitutions, its spirit and words are followed with the right kind of sincerity and honesty. The Tibetan people's respect for and faith in their temporal-cum-spiritual leader is so deep and unalloyed that they try their best to abide by whatever is ordained and expected of them. It may not be wrong to think that the modern, progressive, truly democratic Tibetan society in India is a reflection of that commitment and influence.

But, how did their Constitution-makers get the idea of such an egalitarian socio-political system? Was it because of the ideas they carried in their minds from the post-1951 Tibet, moulded in the Chinese Communist ideology? Or did the already existing egalitarian society of the pre-1959 Tibetans got reflected in the Constitution? I could not manage to get clear answers; but, it seems both can be true. Let us, now, go into the salient features of and the significant messages from the Constitution.

In 1959, when the Dalai Lama sought refuge in India from Chinese oppression, about 80,000 Tibetans followed him into exile. The flow of refugees continued. By 1994, the total number, including those born in exile, had reached 130,000. In the early years there were limited arrangements to keep precise count of the refugees settled in far-flung camps in India and elsewhere. The central Tibetan exile administration is in close touch with the entire community now. In 1994, 104,686 of the exiles were in India, 15,000 in Nepal, 1,457 in Bhutan and 4,634 in Switzerland and North America. They are now, by and large, an educated, self-reliant community.

The long period of exile is being spent in places with very different climatic and cultural conditions from their homeland. But they are linked by institutions of democratic self-government and the commitment to return to Tibet. The personality of the Fourteenth Dalai Lama, their spiritual and temporal head, has provided them with additional binding.

At the same time, his self-programmed reduction of his temporal powers has induced a kind of confidence in democracy. The vision of the exiled diaspora is no longer focussed exclusively on his person. It is the Assembly of Tibetan Deputies (parliament-in-exile) in Dharamsala that is delineating their future.

The Dalai Lama keeps inspiring and encouraging his people to educate themselves and their children so that they can be of service to their society here, as well as in Tibet where they will ultimately return. The Parliamentary form of self-government here (in exile) is meant to be a model for their new political system in Tibet. Less than a year after seeking refuge in India, the Dalai Lama outlined a programme designed to introduce the exiles to the practice of democratic self-rule, without losing touch with their own traditions. He chose to make the announcement in January,1960 in Bodh Gaya, where Lord Buddha attained enlightenment thus emphasising the historical, cultural and religious linkages between Tibet and India.

The process was accelerated in 1990, when the Assembly of the Tibetan Peoples' Deputies i.e. their Parliament, was expanded and given independent authority. Membership of 13 in the First Assembly (1960) went up to 17 in the Tenth (1988). It was empowered to elect the Kashag (Cabinet) consisting of seven Kalons (ministers), who were made responsible to the Assembly. Until then, appointing the Kalons was the exclusive prerogative of the Dalai Lama. The change has given substance to the proceedings of the Assembly, where the Kalons now find themselves defending and explaining the working of the Executive before a critical House. As noted by a senior official, some Kalons complain that when the Deputies, now, need clarification, they no longer go up to the Kashag (situated physically above the

Assembly), but summon the Kalons to come down.[1]

The change has had far-reaching repercussions. The Deputies now discuss and lay down policies on issues that were formerly the preserve of the Dalai Lama and his advisers. They keep a close watch on foreign relations and the activities of Tibetans abroad. This has made a crucial difference to policies towards China also.

The first steps towards educating the Tibetan exiles in democratic procedures were taken soon after the first wave of refugees arrived in India. The Dalai Lama had, in fact, initiated the process of democratization in Tibet itself before being forced to flee to India. In his autobiography, My Land and My People, he recalls how he appointed a Reforms Committee of eminent citizens to redress the inequalities prevailing in Tibet, but the reforms were obstructed by the Chinese occupation. In his Foreword to the Constitution for Tibet drafted in 1963, the Dalai Lama stated: "Even prior to my departure from Tibet in March 1959, I had come to the conclusion that in the changing circumstances of the modern world, the system of governance in Tibet must be modified and amended as to allow the elected representatives of the people to play a more effective role in guiding and shaping the social and economic policies of the State. I also firmly believed that this could only be done through democratic institutions based on social and economic justice."[2]

In January 1960, at Bodh Gaya (where Lord Buddha achieved enlightenment), he outlined a detailed programme to a large body of Tibetans gathered there. It was there that he advised them to set up an elected body with three exile representatives for each of the three cholkhas and one each for the four religious sects. Elections were duly held and the first elected representative body in Tibet's history took office on September 2, 1960. This historic day continues to be observed by the Tibetan community ever since as Democracy Day.[3]

The Deputies took time to realize their responsibilities, preferring to leave supervision of the infant exile administration to the Dalai Lama and the Kalons appointed. In his address to the assembled Deputies and other eminent Tibetans in Dharamshala on May 11,1990, the Dalai Lama announced, "From now on, the people's decision will be final. I feel that the Dalai Lama should have no role here. The future assembly will be entrusted with the power of appointing the Kalons." He then declared the existing Tenth Assembly dissolved. He also outlined proposals for expanding membership of the Assembly and giving more representation to women. He spoke of the need of a judicial tribunal to look into citizen's complaints. On May 29, 1991, the Dalai Lama had the satisfaction of addressing the 11th Assembly of Tibetan Peoples Deputies, the outcome of his epoch-making pronouncement the previous year. Its membership had risen from 12 to 46 to represent all sections of the exile community in India and abroad, including the religious sects. There are 10 deputies each from the three major provinces (rather, from the people, originally belonging to those provinces) of Utsang, Amdo & Kham, 2 from Europe, 1 from North America, 2 members each from 5 religious sects and 3 members nominated by the Dalai Lama. The voting age was fixed at 18 years and the minimum age for contesting election at 25 years.

"When we first came into exile in 1959," he told the Assembly, "we decided that the future Tibet would move with the times while retaining the virtues of our traditional value system. We decided that although we would borrow the attributes of the modern world, we would retain our own traits, which are appreciated even by the outsiders. With this in mind, we made efforts towards the democratization of our community through measures like the election of the members of the Assembly of Tibetan Peoples Deputies. We decided that the democratic reforms thus introduced should be documented in writing so that in future there would be clear-cut guidelines and a basis for further thinking and improvement. We started working on this in 1961 and promulgated a draft democratic constitution in 1963. Of course, the *ultimate decision as to whether to adopt, amend or reject this constitution is left in the hands of the Tibetan people* when we are united in Tibet in future."[4]

On February 26, 1992, he set forward what were described as "Guidelines for Future Tibet's Polity and the Basic Features of the Constitution." His vision and plans for the future is best conveyed in his own words—

"I believe that in future Tibet should have a multi-party system of parliament, and that should have three organs of government, namely legislature, executive and judiciary, with a clear separation of powers between them, each independent of the other and vested with equal powers and authority. As I have often said, Tibet belongs to Tibetans, and *especially to those who are in Tibet*. Therefore, Tibetans in Tibet shall bear the main responsibility in future Tibet's democratic government. Moreover, Tibetan officials presently serving the government of Chinese-occupied Tibet should bear even greater responsibility in running the affairs of state".[5] In a subtle manner, the Dalai Lama is drawing our attention to the improbability of retur ning to Tibet.

As for himself, the Dalai Lama reiterated: "Personally, I have made up my mind that I will not play any role in the future government of Tibet, let alone seek the Dalai Lama's traditional political position in the government". To reassure the Tibetans, however, he stated: "I am determined to do whatever I can for the well-being of my people....I will, most likely, remain a public figure who may be called on to offer advice or resolve some particularly significant and difficult problems which could not be overcome by the existing government of political mechanisms. I think I will be in a better position to serve the people as an individual outside the government."

He reiterated his intention to withdraw even further from governmental responsibility. "I have made up my mind that I will not be the head of, or play any role in, the government when Tibet becomes independent," he said. "The future head of the Tibetan government must be someone popularly elected by the people. Such a step, as I have been saying repeatedly, has many advantages and will enable us to become a true and complete democracy."[6]

This voluntary renunciation of centuries-old absolute and unquestioned power and supreme position (an act, a "phenomenon", that is the first of its kind and is going to remain the "first" for so many more centuries to come) has worked wonders with the Tibetans in exile. They have, without much effort, become true followers of the democratic norms of their Constitution. If the preceding chapters have helped us to understand the Tibetan mind and culture adequately, then it should not be difficult for us to understand that this spontaneous and effortless adherence to the Constitution or a truly democratic norm was as simple and "natural" for them as their unquestioning loyalty was and is to the institution of Dalai Lama. That is why, the Tibetan government-in-exile is the one and the only instance in the history of parliamentary democracy where the Constitution and the system are working word by word, with full respect and allegiance to its true spirit. And, that is why, the Tibetan society in India is an unique gender-equal society.

The thousands of refugees who accompanied and followed the Dalai Lama into exile when he sought refuge in India in 1959 traveled on foot over high mountain passes and endured terrible hardship. They got virtual destitutes suffering the trauma of leaving their homes and finding themselves in a totally different environment. Few were educated and they had no experience of democratic institutions. They got settled on land provided by Indian hospitality but had to earn their livelihood by hard manual labour. Yet, as early as in 1960, the Dalai Lama was able to instil the seeds of self-reliance and democratic norms. The exiled community adapted wonderfully fast and with ease to new conditions, new life-styles and new values & norms. This, soon, became part of their thought process and life-style. Now they are reaping full benefits of the new system; they are one of those rare groups /communities who are contented, peaceful and peace-loving, inspite of being refugees and struggling endlessly for the freedom of their homeland. His Holiness said, on March 20, 1991, during his address to the British House of Commons All-party Parliamentary Group, "this democratisation has reached out to Tibetans all over the world...I believe that the future generation of Tibetans will consider these changes among the most important achievements of our experiences in exile."[7]

The present Dalai Lama had tried similar reforms while in Tibet itself, but backward pull of feudalism and tradition must have been too powerful.Due, mainly, to the topography, the Tibetan civilisation happened to be "cocooned", and, therefore exclusivist and conservationist. By nature the people were contented; there was no observable discontent to call for a change. Besides, their deep religiosity had made them almost incapable of comprehending the values of something new or different. This complete and radical change in their home, hearth, livelihood and life situation could not but radically change their thinking and thought process. Besides, this was the first time (i.e. in exile) that they got exposed to a world / civilisation outside theirs. They realised the immense benefits of accepting the values of modernity.

B

Since this large body of deputies could not be in session for long period, the Tibetan Parliament-in-Exile constituted a Standing Committee consisting of:

a) Two members out of the representative of each region,

b) One member out of the representatives of each religious lineage

c) One member out of the nominees of H.H. the Dalai Lama

The Standing Committee was vested with almost all the functions and powers of the Parliament (ATPD) except in respect to legislative and financial business. The secretariat of the Assembly functions under the charge of a Parliamentary Secretary, who advises the Chairman and provides advice on parliamentary procedures and practices and makes arrangements for recording the formal proceedings of the house.

The Chairman and Deputy Chairman are elected by the members. These two functionaries are vested with the authority to represent the parliament with outside organizations and persons. They preside over the meetings of the Standing Committee as well as other parliamentary committees and are responsible for the administration of the House. The main powers and responsibilities of ATPD are:

* to elect the members of the Kashag (Cabinet) and also to impeach any individual Kalon (minister) or the entire Kashag;

* to enact laws, frame rules and regulations and issue policy decisions;

* to liaise with governments, parliaments, NGOs and individuals throughout the world in order to gain support for the cause of Tibet;
* to streamline the functioning of the local Tibetan Assemblies;
* to oversee the work of BRDL Sub-Committees;
* to debate on issues of national and international importance as well as of local and individual significance;
* to hear public grievances and petitions of Tibetans-in-Exile;
* to monitor the aspiration and problem of the Tibetan people both in and outside Tibet by maintaining consistent touch with them;
* to play role of opposition parties as well under the present circumstances as maintaining an effective control on the Government is not only a matter for the opposition, it is the responsibility of the Parliament as a whole.

The Business routine of the house is transacted in the following manner:

- question hour;
- statements of the Kalons or individual members;
- passage of legislation;
- voting of Grant-in aid and control of public finances;
- zero hour;
- processing of miscellaneous budge; and
- debate on motions or statement.

In the interest of preparing and facilitating the work of the Assembly, members are divided into various committees considering their area of specialization to undertake detailed work on behalf of the House. Thus, Committees carry out a major part of the work done by the Assembly. These are:

- Standing Committee
- Business Advisory Committee
- Committee on Education
- Committee on Health Care
- Committee on Human Rights and Environment
- Committee on Public Accounts
- Committee on Religious and Cultural Activities
- Committee on Social Welfare and Settlement; and Select committee on Bills.

The five-year term of the XIth Parliament ended in May 1996 and the XIIth Parliament has been constituted. The first session commenced on 31st May 1996.[8]

Professor Samdhong Rinpoche, Chairperson of the Assembly of Tibetan People's Deputies, wrote in his booklet, "Tibet: A Future Vision", that "freedom in Tibetan language is called `Rangwang.' It is something more than mere translation of the English word `freedom' or `independence'. It is an ancient classical word which meant, precisely, sovereignty, self-control or self-rule. It refers more to self-discipline rather than uncontrolled anarchy. Ultimate freedom is the state of enlightenment without any bondage of karma and klesha (deeds and mental defaults). Seeds of bondage are reversible and eradicable. To achieve such a freedom, a person needs conducive social and geographical environment within which the person's mind could flower in goodness and experience the awakening of the unconditioned intelligence. That requires a conducive inner and outer state where the person's basic potential could be developed in its natural form.[9] This statement is extremely revealing— explaining, most competently, how & why the "traditions" of Tibetan. culture helped in the easy adaptation to the truly liberating "modern" value system.

The following are a few salient and striking features of the Tibetan Constitution—

(i) The future Tibet is conceived as a compact society insulated from divisive forces, be it gender, caste, creed, class, clan, religious denominations, etc. Political, economic and other systems and institutions evolved in free Tibet will discourage any form of groupism detrimental to the integrative character of the society. The basic social fabric of the country shall be woven around the spirit of harmony, love and care and equality among all the people.

(ii) Since all persons have a right to a decent standard of living for themselves and their families, efforts will be directed to minimize the gap between the rich and the poor, the educated and the uneducated, the city dwellers and the residents of villages and the older and the younger generations, in all possible manner. Wealth, position or status, trade and occupation shall not be the basis of social dignity or hierarchy.

(iii) The entire territory of the country belongs, by natural law, to the citizens of the country. No person can claim individual ownership of earth, air, water, fire and space. Based on this principle, the land of the country shall also be owned by the entire people, but it shall be available to each citizen *according to his need and ability to use it.*

(iv) The root-cause of all divisions, discriminations, strifes, conflicts and age-old oppressions and exploitations is nothing but property (originally, land) and the insatiable greed for its ownership, expressed, more often than not, through violence and inhuman treatment. That is why, primitive (tribal) societies, practicing common /community ownership of land or productive means, are, more or less, egalitarian and peaceful. Do we know of any Constitution or Book of Laws which writes "the entire territory of the country belongs, by natural law, to the citizens of the country (collectively). No person can claim individual ownership of earth, air, water, fire and space"? Have we ever come across any book of ethics or religion which expresses such sentiment or belief ? The words "By natural law" is the most vital part of this law / injunction. If such a core of the core sentiment can be really put into action, then the need for laws, regulations or political authority becomes thoroughly irrelevant.

The human societies, through ages, have created laws and strong socio-political authorities to protect the law-abiding citizens and to punish the law-breakers; religions, also, have been created to serve, more or less, the same purpose. But nobody thought of laws that could *prevent* the occurrence of crimes or make inhuman and anti-human behaviour & practices impossible....The "makers" of laws, civil or religious are the ones who divided land (earth) and other gifts of Nature (viz: air, water, fire & space) into individual ownerships or ownership by those who usurp and wield power to create an atmosphere of fear.

Notable here is, also, the fact that no other book of laws has talked of the immense importance of the facts that (i)human beings are as much part of, and dependent on, Nature as animals, plants and other living beings are, that (ii) perfect harmony with Nature or the correct observance of Nature's laws are absolutely necessary for good living and peaceful atmosphere and that (iii) all the miseries and injustices that the individuals, communities or nations suffer are primarily because Nature is robbed and Nature's balance is disturbed. Thus, the law under discussion can be taken as a foundational law or the law of all laws.

The next part of the Constitutional provision is: "based on this principle. The land of the country shall also be owned by the entire people; but, it shall be available to each citizen according to his *need and ability to use it.* It sounds quite similar to the binding principle of Lenin's Soviet Russia. Did Marx arrive at this principle by observing Nature and its laws? The Dalai Lama says, "in Communism, the original idea came from the motivation that in the human community there is a great gap; there is a conflict between the more privileged community and the less privileged community. It seems that Marxism is concerned with the distribution of wealth. This idea is something very positive & noble. The idea of Marxism is something for the majority and a sacrifice for the minority, and I think this is right."[10] He further observed that a large number of people in Asia are living under Communist regimes and, therefore, he suggests, (i) exploring "common grounds" between the two "isms" and (ii) establishing friendly relations (with the Communist governments). He says, "even in countries where Marxism flourishes, traces of Buddhism are still there. Under these circumstances, I think, some sort of dialogue between Marxism and Buddhism, especially Mahayana Buddhism, will be very beneficial to many people of this region." Appreciating the fundamental value of Communism, the Dalai Lama rightly points out that "real Communism is not created by force, but by voluntary force in helping people to become less selfish....In order to do that, you need tremendous will & determination on the basis of altruism....not by gun...." He feels that the principles & practice of Mahayana Buddhism can help to achieve good socialism.[11]

(v) The Tibetan Constitution-makers felt "in order to present a better & humane alternative to the capitalist economic system, the communists devised & developed the socialist economic system. But, both capitalist & socialist economic systems are unsuitable for the well-being of human society, in general, and for the betterment of the Tibetan society, in particular. Thus, there is no appropriate existing model of economic system for the Tibetan society. The economic policy has to be based on the concept of self-sufficiency and proper apportioning of surplus growth so as to fulfill the requirements of the real needs of the people."[12]

(vi) A self-sufficient economy will mean that the necessities like food, house, clothes and basic medicines are produced in sufficient quantity within the country, preferably at regional and local levels. It does not, however, imply that nothing can or should be imported from outside: it only means that the total national import must be equal to or less than the total export value and that there is no trade deficit. Foreign aid and contributions may be accepted after carefully scrutinizing all aspects. Under no circumstances foreign loan will be accepted, howsoever easy may be the repayment terms and conditions or even if it be interest free.

(vii) Trade through barter system will be encouraged within the country to simplify trading. The role of money and its absolute value, has to be curbed. Money is easy to accumulate, it is easy to steal and it is also very easy to show off.

It is important to take special note of two novel ideas, which we do not find in any other society—primitive or modern, and not even in socialist /communist economic systems, viz: (i) "the role of money and its absolute value has to be curbed, because money is easy to accumulate,easy to steal, and it is also very easy to show off" and (ii) "under no circumstances,foreign loan will be accepted, however easy may be the repayment terms & conditions and even if it is interest-free".These show how deeply genuine is their love for freedom at both national and individual levels; these, also, show their concept of socialism and anti-imperialism, born out of their direct experiences with life and Nature, and not out of academic thinking and activism. Such concepts of socialism, equality and freedom are preventive, i.e. stops evil from happening, and not a formula for 'what to do after the mischief is done'.

(viii) The next Constitutional provision stresses, as expected, on the vital importance of Natural environment or eco-system. This too, is born out of their love for equality and freedom. Equality & freedom are dependent on each other; one cannot exist without the other and one cannot be realised without the other. Equality and freedom or, in other words, perfect balance in human life & civilization cannot be achieved and maintained unless the desired balance in Nature is maintained. Tibetan economy is planned to ensure the maintenance and protection of ecological balance. Ecological degradation results from greed and mindless exploitation of natural resources. The Tibetan Constitution talks of management of land and its use in a scientific manner by equitable, proportionate distribution of forest area, grazing area, agricultural land, horticulture area, housing, small private gardens, etc. Industrial area will be located and developed separately, away from habitats — both urban and rural. Traditional handicrafts, cottage industries and small scale industries will be encouraged and given priority. Future Tibet will not join any international finance or trade organization and in the interest of its own countrymen shall maintain a neutral policy. However, Tibet shall have bilateral mutually advantageous trade relations with other countries, particularly its neighbours like India, Nepal, Bhutan, China, Mongolia and others. Its policy will be that of caution towards the introduction of heavy machinery which is supposed to be time-saving, labour-saving, etc. *Machine will not decide the fate of men; men will always control the machines*.

(ix) Of the many benefits the Tibetans happened to derive from their life in exile, like a modern democratic Constitution and a gender-equal & class-neutral socio-political system, universal secular education was most significant; their deepest gratitude to the host government is because of the widespread opportunities created for their education. In fact, the teaching standard, the facilities and the maintenance of the Tibetan Central Schools are far better than the Central Schools meant for the children of Defence personnel and other Central Government officers of India. The Tibetans neither knew, nor could think of, any such education system while in Tibet. They do not accept that such facilities were opened up under the Chinese occupation. These exiles, with a new-found identity, have also realised that the new-found democratic and progressive ideas are the gifts of this education system and their educated minds.

C

This Tibetan experience is a very good example of what education can do. Education is the most effective tool for a radical transformation in a society. This should be an excellent motivation for our governments which are disregarding Article 14 of our Constitution,i.e. free & *compulsory* education for all till the age of 14, shamelessly for the last 48 years! In this regard, it is worth quoting from the Tibetan Constitution that "any absence from basic schooling will be punishable under law for parents who are found guilty of not sending their children to schools."The other provisions, related to education, *binding* both for the government and the citizens, are mentioned below.

The main objective of the education policy of 'Future Tibet' shall be to develop the minds of young Tibetans in a manner that they regain their originality and unfold their basic potential in goodness and awakening of intelligence.

This may be termed as natural flowering. The aim of education will not be merely to earn livelihood or obtain gainful employment but much more than that. The purpose of human life is to attain supreme freedom and in that process to lead a blissful and holistic life for which dispelling of ignorance and awakening of wisdom are indispensable. Education will be instrumental only in giving an individual the *ability to inquire into everything without any pre-conceived notion.* Education will be given top priority in the national agenda and not less than one-fifth of the annual budget of the central and the state governments combined will be allocated for the purpose. In order to attract talent, the social status and service conditions of teachers shall be the highest among all the professions. Commercialization and elitism in education will not be permitted. Service conditions and salaries also should be good.

(x) No Tibetan citizen of school-going age will be allowed to remain without proper schooling except those who are duly admitted as monks or nuns in a recognized monastery or nunnery. Any absence from basic schooling will be punishable under law for parents who are found guilty of not sending their children to schools. Necessary and adequate facilities will be provided by the State for handicapped and disabled children. Entire expenditure on basic school education, including the cost of textbooks, will be borne by the State. Parents will be required to contribute only towards the cost of school dress, transport and stationary. Tibetan language shall be taught compulsorily from pre-school to the Intermediate class. From Class V to VII a foreign language will be taught as an optional subject. The study of classical languages which have profound significance for traditional Tibetan culture will be encouraged. The other compulsory subjects will include Civics, Ethics, Mathematics and General Science. The continuation of family business will be encouraged, the idea being that basic education must not be responsible for turning the recipient into a white-collared worker and delinking him from hereditary family occupation.

(xi) The State shall have only one University established by law, though it may have one or more campus in each province to cater to university education at regional level. The idea behind only one university is to make the firm establishment and observance of basic educational and ethical norms and policies easier and surer.

(xii) Traditional monastic education shall not be governed by the university system.

(xiii) Any courses of study related to warfare, weapon production, or any experiment involving torture of animals will not be permitted in any institution.

(xiv) The topmost priority that the Tibetans attach to the conservation of eco-system or Nature's balance gets, once again, reflected in the laws regarding health & family welfare. To quote from the Constitution, "efforts will be made so as to use water from natural streams or wells. In the event of drinking water through supply system becoming unpotable, proper drinking water will have to be provided by other means. Chemical disinfectants and pest control agencies will be avoided as far as possible. Use of chemical fertilizers and similar other means for agriculture, horticulture and fruit growth will also be avoided. Recycling of garbage for fertilizers will be planned in a manner so as to minimize pollution and tensions." What a correct assessment that pollution necessarily leads to tension. We all know that pollution is created by industrialization and commercialization, causing tension and the most dreadful illness, viz: hypertension.

(xv) The Tibetans own an excellent system of medicine. It works miraculously when Allopathy or Homeopathy fail. It is gaining fast in popularity not only in India but also in parts of Europe & America. Yet, the government has an open mind to the specific benefits of all other systems (including Allopathy). What is important to them is the well-being of the people—whatever is the means. This, once again, shows how genuinely people-oriented this government is. (It is worth mentioning here that the Indian governments, till recently, did not recognise India's own traditional system, viz: Ayurved & Unani, and does not yet recognize the Tibetan system, notwithstanding the fact that a premier research institute (govt.), All India Institute of Medical Science, New Delhi, is engaged in collaborative research on AIDS with the doctors & researchers of the Tibetan Medical & Astro Institute, Dharamshala).

One of the angers that the Tibetans have against the Chinese "occupation" is about the "forced" family planning or the absence of freedom related to the number of children a couple likes to have. Here, too, like in all other matters, they felt that Nature's ways should not be tampered with. But,at the same time, they are not all that orthodox or irrational: they do not consider family planning an evil. They feel, under the circumstances, small families are neither necessary, nor beneficial.The migrants in India like to have as many children as their economic conditions allow because they are few in number. Besides, fertility rate among their women is much lower than in the hot plains of India. Fertility rates are always lower in cold climates.

In ancient or pre-modern Tibet the religious beliefs and marriage customs contributed to natural family planning. It was a firm social custom that the eldest son became a lama and may be quite a few others also. Secondly, polyandry was quite common. It was necessary for the purpose of conserving the limited arable land the highest cold desert of the world could have.Similar socio-economic practices are found in the Kinnaur district of Himachal Pradesh where Buddhism and Tibetan cultural traits have widespread influence.

Geographically it is next door to Tibet. Trade and barter with Tibet is quite regular and accepted as normal.It is more unhindered than on the West Bengal - Bangladesh or North Bengal-Nepal borders.

(xvi) The Tibetan law-makers believe that nothing—not even the best of the laws—should be imposed or forced upon. That becomes contradictory to the fundamental human laws of freedom. There is no taboo or injunction against birth control. It is not considered necessary, keeping in view the small population of the country. However, other issues related with family planning, e.g. higher minimum age for marriage, gap between two children,etc. are taken up and advised.

D

,(xvii) The supreme importance given to *freedom* gets, once again, reflected in the section on Religion. The Tibetans are deeply religious people, their life and civilisation revolves around religion or the basic tenets of Mahayana Buddhism. Yet, their Constitution declares, "freedom of conscience, freedom of religion, as of well as freedom of *not to believe* in any particular religion, shall be the fundamental right of the people, duly guaranteed under the Constitution. The law of the land shall not be guided by any spiritual tradition, scriptures, religious teachings and /or institutions....Secularism in free Tibet would mean that the State would be aware of its empirical limitations and may not interfere in the sphere of spiritual life of the people in general, and the individuals in particular." But, at the same time,the Constitution says, "the Buddhist way of life provided the best cultural fabric with no fragmentation or discrimination of any kind."

(xviii) Culture in any society or in any community is intimately connected with religion, tradition and history. So, a book of law, guiding the present and the future of a nation has to lay down certain guiding principles on culture. Its best definition perhaps, is written in the section on Culture. "Culture is a state of mind acquired through education and practice of morality, which is the source of creativity....Freedom, natural growth and the flowering of individual mind shall be considered as the basic source of cultural development and no efforts will be spared to preserve traditions, which will ensure this process." A full-fledged Ministry of Cultural Affairs will be set up in "Free Tibet. It will organize archaeological explorations of historical sites and their excavation, preservation of monuments, artefacts, etc. Libraries, museums and archives will be set up at different levels - national, state, district and local - under uniform central legislation. All kinds of handicrafts in metal, wood, stone, textiles, terracotta, etc., shall be promoted. The State would ensure an expenditure of a minimum of 4 per cent out of the nation's budget for preservation, protection and promotion of cultural activities; this would also serve as an effective medium of non-formal education.

(xix) The section on international relations reflects their incorruptible allegiance to non-violence and peace. All stalwarts of power game do talk of peace and non-aggression. But, in reality, they engage in ruthless competition for power and control over others. The Tibetans have every reason to feel violent towards China; yet, their Constitution asserts that "basically, the plan foresees Future Tibet as a "Zone of Ahimsa", implying a demilitarized region, having no alignment with any big power or a power bloc and non-involvement in any kind of the production of arms". The nation's faith in non-alignment, but co-operation, is expressed simplistically and very beautifully. Total absence of any diplomatic language or a language with double /dubious meaning or intent is remarkable. It says, Tibet will not consider any country unfriendly but will always oppose any kind of violation of human rights, suppression of democratic norms, eruption or threat of any violent action, terrorism, religious fanaticism, cultural domination and imposition of language, religious practices and economic and political systems. It is apposed, tooth & nail, to the production and experimentation of nuclear or chemical arms. A variety of political systems and ideologies is desirable to enrich the human community so long as all people are *free to evolve their own political and socio-economic system, based on self-determination*. If people from poor countries are denied the happiness they desire and deserve, they will naturally be dissatisfied and pose problems for the rich. If unwanted imposition by one nation upon another continues, the attainment of world peace is doubtful".

E

(xx) Tibet,according to its Constitution, is specially demarcated not only as a "zone of non-violence", but also as a "sanctuary of environmental preservation". Special care therefore, will be taken to "prevent concentration of population at a few places", to harness "maximum solar energy", to ensure totally undisturbed "maintenance of lakes, ponds, rivers & streams". Strict prohibition of "chemical fertilisers, pesticides & plastic bags,etc." will be enforced. All environmental issues, direct or indirect, will be a matter of serious concern in free and future Tibet. It would be the Govt. of Tibet's goal "to transform Tibet into our planet's largest natural reserve".

(xxi) The "future Tibet" is conceived as a compact society insulated from divisive forces, be it gender, caste, creed, class, clan, religious denominations, etc. Political, economic and other systems and institutions evolved in free Tibet will discourage any form of groupism detrimental to the integrative character of the society. The basic social fabric of the country shall be woven around the spirit of harmony, love and care and equality among all the people.

(xxii) "Since all persons have a right to a decent standard of living for themselves and their families, efforts will be directed to minimize the gap between the rich and the poor, the educated and the uneducated, the city dwellers and the residents of villages and the older and the younger generations, in all possible manner. Wealth, position or status, trade and occupation shall not be the basis of social dignity or hierarchy.

(xxiv) The entire territory of the country belongs, by natural law, to the citizens of the country. No person can claim personal ownership of earth, air, water, fire and space. Based on this principle, the land of the country shall also be owned by the entire people but it shall be available to each citizen according to his need and ability to use it."

References

1. *Tibet's Parliament in Exile* (Tibetan Parliamentary and Policy Research Centre), 1996.
2. Prof. Samdhong Ruipoche (Chairman, Assembly of Tibetan Peoples; Deputies), *Tibet: A Future Vision* (Tibetan Parliamentary and Policy Research Centre, New Delhi),1996.
3. Ajit Bhattacharya, *Tibetans in Exile: The Democretic Vision* (Tibetan Parliamentary and Policy Research Centre, New Delhi) 1994.
4. *op. cit.* 1.
5. *op. cit.* 3.
6. *Dalai Lama—My Land and My People* (Asia Publishing House) 1962.

7. *Life in Exile* (Central Tibetan Relief Committee, Deptt. of Home, Dharamshala, H.P., 1992.
8. *op. cit.* 1.
9. *op. cit.* 2.
10. *op. cit.* 6.
11. *Ibid.*
12. *op. cit.* 2.

6

Position of Women in the Tibetan Society in Exile

Now we come to the main body of our research or to the possible answer to our primary question, viz: what is the socio-economic condition of the Tibetan women living in India as a result of "en masse" migration from their homeland (which was "occupied" by the Chinese communists in 1951).

A

According to a publication from UNHCR, titled "International Migration Policies and the Status of Female Migrants", migrant women, more than men, are important agents of change." M. Tienda & K. Booth make an eye-opening remark in their joint paper presented in a conference at Oslo in June,1988, titled "Migration, Gender and Social Change:a review and reformulations." They wrote,"migration can be viewed as a move between gender stratification systems. But, whether such move improves or erodes women's position will have to be examined empirically on the basis of concrete situations. The research challenge is to identify what aspects of the gender stratification system are similar or different between countries of origin and destination; and more importantly, which of them impinge directly on the status of female migrants." The authors further felt that "migrants can be viewed as embodying the interactions between the norms and attitudes determining female status in sending and receiving countries. Such interactions are dynamic, meaning that the status of female migrants are subject to change.The longer their residence in the country of destination and the more successful their integration, the more likely it is that their status (or the status of their daughters) may reflect the social norms of the host society."

This happening or trend is natural and desirable not merely of the international migrants but equally of the inter-regional or intranational migrants. The migrants, thus, can (i) win over their griefs and grievances better and (ii) face less resistance or non-acceptance from the local people or the common people of the host country. The history of the Indian nation / civilisation is the story of merging of endless streams of "migrants" (they came as invaders) from various parts of Asia since time immemorable. It is,now, impossible to tell which cultural group is the original inhabitant of this vast land mass, rich with varieties of geographical and anthropological resources.

In the course of our studies, it has been noticed that the Tibetan migrants have managed to adjust admirably well in the land of their exile, inspite of the fact that emotionally they have remained ever disturbed for having lost their homeland. They have been like the proverbial swan who is expert in picking up only substance from amidst the muck scattered in the water...The society (in exile) does not "reflect the social norms of the host society." Their government-in-exile has copied the Constitution of the host country in their law making and the citizens abide by them strictly and seriously; they have truly imbibed its spirit. Thus, equality in every sphere is not only a norm but is also in practice (with all sincerity). Gender equality observed in this society is unbelievable, unique and can serve as a model for any society. This is the reason why I developed immense interest in this kind of an investigation/ book.

The autonomy to decide whether to migrate or not, and under what circumstances, as well as the ability to influence the migration decision is itself an important indication of woman's status. In most cases,the greater her subordination to male authority the stronger is her motivation to migrate, although her ability to do so is highly restricted. One important reason for migration (that does not apply to men) is the desire to escape the constraints of subordinate position. Associated with that is the lure of "new" life, which is hoped & expected to be always better as it offers the possibility of economic independence..."the *freedom & independence* of poorly paid work, even".[1]

It is not known, nor did it come out clearly from the interviews or conversations with the women in various settlements, if they had the freedom to decide about migration, but there is no doubt about the fact that these women "escaped the constraints of subordinate positions" by migrating or by coming out of an archaic, stagnant feudal socio-economic system, which, by its very nature, had to be gender unequal /oppressive. There is also no doubt about the fact that the "new" life gave them complete economic independence and the necessarily consequent confidence and gender equality.The Tibetans in India gained everything. What they lost, along with their motherland, was the degenerate feudal system fit to be discarded. They also lost the rule by the ecclesiastical and feudal lords. It was no self-rule. What they got in exile is democratic socialism or true self-rule. The women were real gainers...they had "nothing to lose but their chains."

In this context it is important to bring our reader's attention to the fact that in almost all cases of migration, whether intra-national or international, the migrant's, particularly the woman's, position in the host region or host country is pathetic; they are treated with no humane consideration or human values. Rita Simon & Caroline Brettel points out in their edited book, "International Migration :the Female Experience" [Rowman & Allanheld, New Jersey,1986],that "double discrimination" and "threefold oppression" of female migrants take place- (i) as females, (ii) as migrant workers and (iii) as foreigners or asylum seekers.

A.V. Arakeri, in his exhaustive book on the first Tibetan refugee-settlers in India, borrows a rather useful term from anthro-sociology. He aptly describes the process of rehabilitation of refugees as "cultural transplantation". The unique case of the Tibetans can perhaps be described as cultural regeneration or cultural re-creation. They gifted themselves with a new society and new ideas for governance. Let us now delve into the details of their adjustments, transplantations and creations.

B

The settlers had not only to cope with the language and cultural pressures from the local residents of the host country, but also with the Tibetans from the other regions of Tibet, varying vastly in dialect, custom,etc. The Welfare Officers, that is why, arranged frequent interactions among them through cultural & sports activities. But the most effective way of interaction and integration was through business or work together, e.g.traveling and residing together to sell woollens,etc. New Year celebration and the visits of His Holiness are other very good avenues for this kind of interaction. The best mode of integration among themselves have been through their passion for Tibet's freedom and the benefits of their democratic government and egalitarian social system. According to Arakeri, the change or the new system was necessary and conducive to adjust better in the "transplanted" situation. "The migration of the people from one ecological niche to the other and transplanting them into another cultural set up brings many changes in their culture."[2]

They had to accept and get adjusted to locally available food items, like rice and maize. Wheat became their staple food in place of barley, cow & buffaloes' milk in place of Yak's, grain-oils in place of Yak's butter and more vegetables in place of animal protein, etc. The refugees had to experience new types of diseases and health problems; and inspite of having an extremely developed medicine system (which is working wonders with their Indian patients in many parts of this country), the settlers are taking on to the modern Allopathic treatments available in the local hospitals as well as in the health centres opened for them. Quite a few seek education in the normal Indian schools and try to go to the "developed" West, even though the host government has made very good arrangements for latest secular education, with equal and adequate attention to the retention and encouragement of their culture, in the Tibetan Central Schools. We can perhaps, call this process "acculturation". It implies *exchange* of cultural elements /traits. But, there was no imbibing of Tibetan culture by the local Indians. Secondly, there was no assimilation at all...unlike in case of hundreds of other migrants who have flooded the Indian soil for thousands of years and now constitute the Indian population. The story of the Darjeeling district is different because the Tibetans have been living there for generations, their forefathers having migrated a few generations ago as traders & merchants. They have became part of local population and are considered so by the latter. As a contrast, in and around the refugee settlements the local Indians are not very hospitable; they are even hostile sometimes.

A good number of these Indians are refugees of 1947, i.e. when India gat partitioned. They feel jealous as they did not get that amount of benefits, (as the Tibetans are getting) from the Govt. of India inspite of being Indians. The tribes of Arunachal Pradesh, where a good number of Tibetan camps are scattered, are also not friendly. Historically they have been "neglected" by the Indian government and the mainstream population. Therefore, they feel "alienated" like quite a few other North-east Indian tribes. Development work has also been minimal in those areas. Culturally also they feel suppressed. The Tibetans, in spite of being non-Indians, did not have to suffer any victimisation.

The Tibetan refugees had suffered terrible physical and mental torture during their long journey through very difficult and dangerous mountain routes, but were extremely lucky to reap the benefits of (i) age-old cultural association and affinity with the people of the country where they took asylum, (ii) Indian government's unfriendly attitude towards China and (iii) the general world view of condemnation of China's "territorial ambitions" and ideological imperialism. Tibet was "occupied" by PRC or Communist China in 1951; but the Dalai Lama and the rich & powerful officials and the feudal lords decided to "run away" after 8 long years (1959), when they realised that they had failed miserably in their struggle to resist loss of power. The fate of the Tibetan refugees in India would have been not so favourable if they had sought refuge in 1951 itself when it was the emotional period of "Hindi-Chini bhai bhai", the Bandung Conference and the "Panchsheel". They came at a time (I am not sure if planned or co-incidental) when the Sino-Indian relations had started getting sour and PRC's expansionism was questioning the McMohan Line, which had been arbitrarily drawn by the interests of British imperialism. So, "asylum to the victims of enemy's aggression" strategically suited Indian foreign policy. It also helped India in promoting her image in the South Asian region as the 'big brother'....The world powers, led by U.S.A.,also condemned China and supported the Tibetans and all those countries which offered asylum. That is why, Govt. of India not only did everything best for them, but offered even vast tracts of land and all other facilities for setting up a government of their own ! Has any "host" country, before or after, allowed a 'government of their own' to the refugees? It is like two governments within the same political boundary. The Govt. of India did it as a very effective rebuff to a government,which was both a potential and real threat at that time. It was also to help build up "public opinion" in the world bodies.

C

A kind of caste system, based on occupation (philosophically similar to the Indian) existed in Feudal Tibet. That facilitated the social divisions necessary to retain feudal power effectively.[Kindly refer back to Chapter 2].The Tibetans belonging to the 6th.,7th. & 8th. divisions did not own any landed property. Like the Shudras in India, they functioned as service classes and had to rush to the needs of the higher /privileged /landed classes. In return they received money and/or food and clothing on some occasions. The notion of purity of blood (like in the Indian caste system) prohibited them from marrying outside their endogamous unit. As mentioned earlier, there was a dramatic change in their land-holding pattern (after setting in India). Land for livelihood was distributed by the Govt. of India, according to their need or the size of the family. This automatically brought equality in their socio-economic structure and consequently, changed their age-old mindset and power structure. These "new" land-owning farmers did not "inherit" the land; it had to be surrendered back to the government in case of death of the owner-farmer. The Settlement Officer then, re-allocated the land to the ex-owner's son/ daughter / children or anybody else in the household who is interested. It may not be the same land or of the same size or fertility. It may also happen that the "successors" have adopted a different profession; so many families have changed their "occupation" patterns having lost their feudal identities.

Some of the farmers took to trading or carpet-making and a few craftsmen got attracted to farming! By one stroke of brush as if, class, caste and all forms of division and inequality got wiped off. The modern/ secular education system, effectively provided by the Govt. of India (mentioned earlier),immensely helped this process of true democracy and equality. And, gender equality was found to be the most beneficial success. The present Dalai Lama advised that *all* should work with *equal* strength for their community *as a whole*, and ultimately, for the liberation of their country. "The consciousness of the Tibetans regarding the maintenance of traditional family, its property, its name and purity of blood through descendants is now shifted to the maintenance of their own individual families with their own independent occupations."[3]

The Dalai Lama advised the old generation to try to "understand and reconcile."...But, as the old saying goes, "old habits die hard." It was quite a common sight in Mundgod (one of the earliest settlements) that the local (Indian) poor or landless was made to work hard on the lands of the Tibetan "landlords"! Arakeri had not inquired deeper. It could be possible that the Tibetans, indulging in such retrogressive practice, were feudal lords while in Tibet.

D

Life in Exile

It is believed by the Tibetans and their supporters &

sympathisers that they left their country due to the following reasons:

* They had been active in peaceful demonstrations or had spoken out against Chinese oppression and faced political persecution; had often suffered long prison sentences or torture;
* They wish to practise their religion freely without persecution.
* They firmly believe that they can do more to help free their country if they live outside Tibet and collect money and mould world opinion in their favour.
* Children are either sent or brought out of Tibet by their parents for the sake of an education which they believe is absent in the Tibetan Autonomous Region.
* Young people between the ages of 14 and 25 come in search of Western education and business. They see more money and freedom in that.

In 1968 His Holiness the Dalai Lama stated:

> "We have been compelled to take refuge in a foreign country because we were no longer able to enjoy the rights that belong to our people. A foreign power, that had no right whatsoever,occupied our country. In order to preserve our culture, religion, race and traditions, we have taken refuge in a foreign country. It is of vital importance to us to strive to work for the effective realization of the cause. As we cannot always live and depend upon others' charity, we are making our utmost efforts to become self-reliant and at the same time, implement measures for the preservation of our beliefs and culture as far as is possible with the facilities that are available to us."

The majority of the refugees live in India, Nepal & Bhutan, though there are Tibetans in 28 other countries, spread mostly over the rich world of the West like U.S.A., Canada, Australia, Switzerland & France. According to the sources of the Tibetan Govt. in India, approximately 1.2 million Tibetans (around one sixth of the total population) have died through political persecution, execution, torture and starvation. Over, 6,000 monasteries, nunneries and other ancient religious and cultural centers have been destroyed. Tibet has been flooded by Chinese people and there are now 7.5 million Chinese to the 6 million Tibetans living in Tibet.[4]

In 1959, following the Lhasa Uprising and "the subsequent suppression by the Chinese", His Holiness the Dalai Lama left Tibet to seek political asylum in India. Shortly after, a massive flood of around 85,000 Tibetans poured into India and Bhuttan. They made the grueling journey through the Himalayan passes at an attitude of 16,000 feet; many, especially women and children, died on the way.[5]

The total number of Tibetan refugees stands at over 109,500. Of these 106,438 are living in India, Nepal and Bhutan. There are 53 settlements: 35 in India, 11 in Nepal and 7 in Bhutan. These accommodate a total of 66,599 people, which accounts for 63% of the Tibetan refugee population in these countries. According to their main source of income, the settlements can be divided into agricultural, agro-industrial and handicraft-based settlements.[6]

The century-old tradition of carpet weaving proved to be the most successful industrial enterprise and many of the so-called agro-industrial settlements still concentrate on the production of carpet and other handicrafts. The principal handicraft is that of carpet-weaving and in the settlements where it is practised, this is an important source of income. Women in all societies seem to be liking weaving as a good alternate source of income/ livelihood. This is as effective a source of income for new arrivals and those who do not have higher education. A great many Tibetans - just under a third of the total working population in the settlements - are involved in sweater-selling. This started in the early 1960s when Tibetan women started selling homemade woollen sweaters at local bazaars. It proved to be lucrative. Now the Tibetans buy machine-made sweaters, in wholesale, from the Indian factories in Punjab. Many Tibetans travel for three or four months every winter to sell them in the major cities of India. For some this has become a round-the-year activity.

The farmers in the first settlements were given one acre of land each, but as a result of the population increase, the average plot of land is now approximately half an acre per person. Maize, paddy, wheat and potatoes are all important crops but ragi, soya beans, mustard and barley are also grown. The majority of agricultural settlements are situated in South and Central India, although some crops, such as apples, are grown only in the North. The remainder of the population is divided between the service industry (such as running hotels and restaurants), trading (such as private carpet businesses or handicraft shops) and other occupations (such as government jobs).

E

Position of Women

In feudal Tibet the status of women varied according to her socio-economic status (i.e.family occupation), her age and "relational" position in the family. Mothers and mothers-in-law enjoyed the highest status and power. Notwithstanding strict class-caste divisions & stark inequality in feudal Tibet, the position of women were not so unequal. A Tibetan girl is reared with love and affection by her parents. She is allowed to mix freely with boys in their community. She gets equal right to inherit family property. In case of absence of male child in the family she is entitled to the entire family property and prescribed to marry matrilocally.

A woman has the duties of cooking, house keeping and rearing children. They also have an important role to play in the economic activity of the family. She is equally active in spinning, weaving cloth and carpets, working on the farm - in sowing, weeding, harvesting, threshing and transporting the corns and hay. She can easily carry paddy bags on her back like men, even upto a long distance.

When important matters concerning the family are discussed, she joins and her opinions are considered with due respect. With the advance of age a Tibetan woman acquires higher status in society. Tibetans address any elderly woman with a respectful term - A-ma, meaning mother. If she is of equal age she is referred to as A-cha-la (respectful sister). Younger girls are referred to as pu-mp, meaning daughter.

Women play a more important role in Tibetan socio-religious ceremonies. On the New Year's Day they visit all their relatives and exchange gifts. Together with women belonging to the locality, kin and ethnic background they sing and dance. On festival days and on full moon days they sing and dance with male members of their groups. When men dance for recreation and to pass time after the harvest period, women join freely with them and dance through night.

They wield considerable influence as wives and mothers in their conjugal houses. In Tibetan society, the women, once married into another family, do not visit their natal family frequently. When they visit for festivals or rites, they stay for a day or two and usually not more. The first and the subsequent child births also take place at their conjugal family. As daughters-in-law they have important roles to play in their daily life. Right from her childhood days she is advised by her family to bear good manners so that there will be no conflict among her conjugal family members. It is quite like in India and China. Woman is the centre of familial activities and her co-operation and willingness is important for the family to continueas a unit. She has to share the domestic work under the close supervision of her mother-in-law and both the mother-in-law and the father-in-law have obligations to take care of their daughter-in-law. They fully understand that she had to come away from her parental family, parting from her consanguineal members in the natal family for ever. The Tibetan woman holds an almost equal status in her natal marital families and plays an important role in decision making. In case of religious rituals she does not enjoy equal status, like the nuns in the Buddhist tradition having lower status than the monks.

These features are quite opposite to what happens in India. The wife is exactly half (*ardhangini*) in status, but equal (*sahadharmini*) in her religious and ritualistic rights and status. In fact, the husband's religious rights remain incomplete without the accompaniment of his wife. King Ram, who is revered as god, had to get a statue of Sita made in gold for performing his royal and religious duties (when he had banished her to the forests).

The age of marriage in Tibetan society, was decided mainly by three factors - physical, social and economic. For girls the age of puberty is taken as the suitable age for marriage; child marriages were not practiced. For marriage, they believe that not only physical but also mental development is necessary. Marriages are arranged late so that the youths will know the meaning and responsibilities of a marriage and also the rules which govern them. They thought this will contribute to stability and happiness in married life. Though the partners had very little choice in traditional society they are now permitted to choose their partners for themselves. They believe that marriages arranged with the consent of the spouses will be more stable.

Tibetans in exile have discarded gender-unequal practices of polygamy and polyandry and other archaic social formations immediately upon leaving their country. But divorces are not as common as it is usually found in societies adopting modern/ secular values. The vices were not imbibed along with the values of a modern society! The greatness about this society (as it has been pointed out earlier also) lies in its remarkable ability about picking up the "desirables" *only* out of a variety of good and bad, and adopting the desirables with equally remarkable speed and efficacy. Divorce,as well as extra-marital sex are thoroughly discouraged and patient and sincere counseling is done to dissuade people from such "deviations"; but no taboos or censuring are imposed. This is a unique society where highest values are attached to an individual's decision-making freedom & power, and the definition of the word "individual" is totally independent of any gender connotation. Family and society, to them, are very sacred, but an individual's freedom is equally sacred. An individual is expected to care for the universally accepted values and norms of his/her society. He/she has been trained and educated so. But the society is also expected to act as his/her friend and not as a dictator. That is why immense value is attached to counseling with patience and perseverance.

The divorced woman does not become the object of gossip or condemnation, nor is she allowed to suffer any emotional & financial problem. The fate of the children i.e. with which parent they would live, is not decided by law or the court; the choice is wholly with the children themselves. They can even change over from one to the other parent whenever they feel like. There is no fixed system of alimony. The woman may support the children even if they are living with their father if she is financially better off. And, with total economic equality and freedom in the society, it may very well happen that the mother is earning more or the father is not earning at all. Lastly, there is no notion of "illegitimate" children in this society. All children are precious and objects of love & care, irrespective of their sex or parentage. This is also because 'motherhood' is worshipped like God; it is considered the best a woman can attain. Yet, infertile or childless women are never looked down upon or deserted.

Though women have equal rights, equal responsibilities and equal position in the family, the presence of father or a father figure in a family is considered necessary and good for the family, particularly for the children. The need for a father or, at least, a father figure is felt because a family is an indivisible whole. This is obvious from the fact that each and every member of a family, irrespective of one's sex or age, has perfectly equal decision making power. Thus, a family is regarded incomplete without the father. There is another reason-quite practical - behind this. However equal and capable women may be, physically they are not as strong as men and therefore, a man's presence is beneficial for the family. It needs protection. Re-marriage is as much encouraged as breaking up of a marriage is discouraged. Because of this reason there is strong counseling against sex or child-birth outside marriage, though there is no notion of a "bastard" or any derogatory position of a single mother or a fatherless child in this society.

On remarriage, the divorced person (man or woman) loses his/ her rights over all movable/ immovable properties of his/ her earlier family.[7]

F

Economic Activities of Women

A Tibetan woman plays a very significant role in the household. The housewife is in charge of every matter of the household. She is even in charge of the family funds. All matters pertaining to the family are discussed among themselves. Even young sons and daughters are consulted in all matters. Among the farmers and nomads, women did almost every type of job. In aristocratic households maid servants were engaged. Women of the middle class did all sorts of household work such as cooking, sweeping, water carrying and the like. The pattern is similar to the Indians'. Both men and women were engaged in cutting down firewood and collecting fuel. But, the Tibetan women perform all duties in the households with an upper hand. It may be due to the reason that Tibetan men generally prefer to remain idle. (This is quite similar to the trend among the hill-people in India). A woman in her home is actually the mistress of the family; her words carry real weight. Women never took part in hunting and trapping though some authors mention about the women of some minority groups of Tibet taking part in hunting and trapping. (As already mentioned before, there was practically no minority group in Tibet. All ethnic groups were of equal political status. These minority groups were living in the areas adjoining Tibet).

Based on the traditional ways and livelihood patterns, Tibetans were divided into 5 main classes of people viz, monks, nobles, traders, farmers and herders. About 90 percent of the population depended on agriculture and animal husbandry. People, who were engaged in small-scale industries, were very few in number and these included carpet weavers and smiths. Some other minor occupations were forestry, hunting, trade and commerce, etc. Several were engaged as labourers. Agricultural productivity was at the subsistence level; but the farmers and nomads never suffered from starvation. They were healthy and sturdy people; their standard of living was higher than that of the people in other parts of under-developed Asia. There was no widespread discontent. Tibetan economy as a whole was self-contained. The land was unproductive due to climatic conditions and poor soil. Sometimes only one crop was grown during the year.

In Tibetan economy, pastoral people played an important role. There were nomadic herders who lived on land which is unsuitable for agriculture. They had grazing pastures and raised animals in small or large herds. During winter they came to lower valleys, while in summer they moved up to high pastures. The herdsmen always lived in groups and owned sheep, yak, dri (female yak), donkeys, mules, horses, etc. Milk, butter, and cheese were obtained from most of these animals. While other animals provided wool. Dris and yaks were most valuable for the Tibetan economy. Mainly women are engaged in the wool industry. It is also a part-time job when they are not busy in agriculture and are free from other things. The finished serge, for example, was used by Tibetans and was also exported for use to other Tibetan ethnic groups living outside Tibet. The second largest cottage industry is carpet-making. Tibetan rugs and carpets are very popular in the Western homes. It is said that the carpets made in Tibet at present are of an inferior quality compared to those prepared by Tibetans living in exile in Nepal and India. In carpet-making, a majority of the workers are women.

The third type of cottage industry, which is very popular, is the making of ornaments, Buddhist images, portable-shrines, mini-cylinders, mini-stones, musical instruments, khata (scarf), hand-printed religious books, amulets, wooden cups and other ritual objects. Women, earlier, were not involved. This cottage industry was in the hands of Newari craftsmen who had either settled in Lhasa or were hired by Tibetan traders.

Tibetan people as a whole, were and are, self-supporting and self-reliant. Before its Chinese occupation there was no developmental planning in Tibet. Only during the regime of the 13th Dalai Lama i.e. during 1876-1993, some progressive measures were adopted; but they were not successful. Tibet is quite rich in minral wealth. It is described that gold dust is found in river-beds of many Tibetan rivers but they were not mined due to the superstitious belief that to do so is against religion.Gold leads to property, greed and deception.We know how their religion and even the present democratic Constitution rule against these. In Tibet, borax, soda, rock-salt, silver, limestone, iron, lead, coal, uranium, etc. exist but mining was not done. In the exploitation of mineral wealth, women had almost no role.

The export items were wool carpet, yak-tail, borax, salt, medicinal herbs, animals and animal products, etc. Business took place on a barter system. In these trades merchants and traders also included women "who sometimes do a good job."[8] Tibetans are good businessmen. Women traders, though they were not many in number, were equally competent and prosperous. In exile, business seems to be more in the hands of women. But in Darjeeling, where Tibetans had come many generations back as traders, women are not in greater number in business. Retail business is mainly controlled by women. A majority of the Tibetans belong to the middle class; none of them fall into the category of the poor.

A majority of the persons who were agriculturists in native Tibet have switched over to business while the rich or the noble class (of the native Tibetan society) are in the

Tibetan administration of the Dalai Lama. Some agriculturists of the native society are also working as labourers in the Border Security Force of India. Some are employed in private enterprises or are earning their subsistence by working in traditional crafts. Those Tibetans, who were herdsmen in the native society have mostly taken to business. Those living in big settlements, especially in South India, are exclusively working as agriculturists. However, their mode of farming has changed from the traditional to modern. They are more or less maintaining the status, prestige and standard of living which they originally had.

In the changed condition even monks are choosing self-support and some are running cottage industries in cooperation with laymen. The Tibetans in exile have adjusted themselves to the changed conditions & there is no business rivalry with local people except in some big Tibetan settlements. In Nepal, Tibetans have trained and engaged several thousand Nepalese in the trade of carpet-weaving. In the pre-1959 settlements of Darjeeling district, Nepalese are employed as domestic servants by the well-to-do Tibetans.

Tibetan women are an extraordinary driving force. They are energetic, hardworking and confident. Sample of a day's work schedule of a woman farmer:

From	To	Activities
5.00 A.M.	5.30 A.M.	Grinding *Ney* for tsampa and wheat, etc.
5.30 A.M.	6.00 A.M.	Looking after cattle, washing and cleaning
6.00 A.M.	6.30 A.M.	Drinking butter tea and eating tsampa.

6.30 A.M.	7.00 A.M.	Milking the cows, feeding the animals
7.00 A.M.	8.00 A.M.	Making lunch. Boiling milk, making curds, (Lunch includes boiled meat, momo, etc.)
8.00 A.M.	12.00 Noon	Working in the filed.
12.00 Noon	1.00 P.M.	Eating Lunch
1.00 P.M.	5.00 P.M.	Working in the filed.
5.00 P.M.	5.15 P.M.	Return from the field.
5.15 P.M.	5.30 P.M.	Milking animals. cattle, sheep goats, etc.
5.30 P.M.	6.00 P.M.	Making dinner Thupa with yak meat or mutton
8.00 P.M.	9.00 P.M.	Dinner (Momo & Curry)
9.00 P.M.	9. 30 P.M.	Recitation of prayers and puja by elderly women of the family
10.00	10.30 P.M.	Boiling milk, preparation of curds, butter, etc.
10.30 P.M.		Retire to bed.

A day's sample working schedule of a typical Tibetan woman carpet weaver:

From	To	Activities
5.30 A.M.	6.00 A.M.	Washing, cleaning.
6.00 A.M.	6.30 A.M.	Worshiping and reciting of preliminaries especially by elderly women.
6.30 A.M.	7.00 A.M.	Butter Tea/Breakfast

7.00 A.M.	8.00 A.M.	Weaving for extra earning.
8.00 A.M.	12.00 Noon	Working in the factory.
12.00 Noon	1.00 P.M.	Lunch/Butter Tea.
1.00 P.M.	8.00 P.M.	Working in factory.
8.00 P.M.	9.00 P.M.	Some work extra time to earn more
9.00 P.M.	10.00 P.M.	Cooking & eating dinner, Gossiping among peers.
10.00 P.M.		Retire to bed.

They are very good at running restaurants of Tibetan & Chinese cuisine. They are also doing prosperous business in "hing" (ferula asafoetida),"shilajit"(bitumen or asphalt) and "kasturi" (musk)-famous Tibetan products of immense medicinal value and of Asia-wide demand. Their typical jwellery of semi-precious stones fetch them fabulous income from the tourists, particularly those from the Western world.

The principal handicraft is that of carpet-weaving and it is an important source of income, particularly for those women who do not and cannot go for higher education. A great many Tibetans, about a one-third of the total working population, are involved in sweater-selling. It is so lucrative that their own production of woollens is not able to cope up with the demand. So they are also selling machine-made sweaters bought from Ludhiana (Punjab). These women travel all over India to sell these woollens. The local customers prefer buying their woollens from the Tibetans because those sold by the Tibetans have got associated with excellently things warm Typical Tibetan woollens are hand-made and with natural dyes; so the waranth and the softness of wool is preserved.

The occupation next in importance is farming. (But

it is so only in the settlements in the plains and the South, not so much in the Himalayan region, which is the focus of my study). Originally they were given one acre of land each. It now works out to half an acre per head (due to rise in population).Maize, paddy, wheat and potatoes are the most important crops, but ragi, soya beans, mustard and barley are also grown. Apples and other hill fruits are grown in the mountain settlements.

The next important means of livelihood is running hotels and restaurants, carpets and handicrafts shops. Quite a good number of the educated are engaged in teaching and government jobs. Tibetans with Indian citizenship are in the Indian Defence Services in quite a large number.

Educational facilities, starting from pre-primary upto Class XII are universal and in great demand. About 25,000 children attend 84 Tibetan Schools in India, Nepal and Bhutan. Of the 92% attending school in various settlements in exile about 84% go to the special schools meant for them, viz: Tibetan Central Schools.

The Special Role of The Nuns

We are already aware of the special position of religious principles and religious persons in the life, psyche and the very existence of a typical Tibetan. They see no contradiction between a secular Constitution with a perfectly class-equal and gender-equal society, on the one hand, and deep religiosity of an ordinary Tibetan with deep faith in Dalai Lama and deep regard for the monks and the nuns on the other.

It is difficult for an Indian to understand this. In India a religious person is normally superstitious, obscurantist and a fanatic,believing in all kinds of divisions and discriminations between man and man, and man and woman.

The Tibetans regularly donate a good sum of their income to the monasteries and consider it a necessary duty (though it is voluntary and there are no laws or orders related to that). "Nunnery is like a lotus flower resting calmly on the troubled waters of worldly life, with its roots firmly anchored in the ground beneath the swamps of cyclic existence; may it also be a source of strength and inspiration for many lay persons."[10]

There was an additional and a very special reason behind the reverence and admiration of the common people for the nuns; it was because of their fearless patriotism and utter selfless sacrificefor their country ever since 1951 (and, it is said, till to this day). The interview given by Mrs. Topping is worth quoting here. "One of the living Buddhas who came to talk with us was a woman, a former nun named Doujemabo. She was an attractive woman who wore her long hair pulled back except for a fringe of bangs across her high forehead. She had pleasing, even features and a Madonna smile. A green Chinese jacket almost covered her pink silk blouse worn with a black Tibetan tunic and a traditional apron. A yellow scarf, the colour of purity, was draped loosely around her neck."[11]

It is described that she was forcibly taken away by the armed supporters of His Holiness, the 14th Dalai Lama. The band rode until their horses died. She reached India after a 2 month journey, and after living there for 4 months she came back to Tibet with a small group. It is said that the Chinese so much 'brain-washed' her that she renounced priesthood and was married. When she was having a priestly role, her name was Samdhing Forjee Phagmo. She later became a delegate to the National People's Congress in Peking.

The first-hand descriptions of her priestly and married

lives were made available to Ms. Topping by a few persons whom she interviewed. According to an informant in 1987, Samdhing is living in Lhasa. At present, her age is about 46 years. She now denies that she had any priestly role. Now she never likes to be called a living goddess. She is now against Lama theocracy. According to her, now she is politically active and is working for the future of Tibet. Her monastic life was as a result of force and her ignorance. The priestly order of Tibet, she feels, was always against new ideas and alien views.[12]

References

1. M.S. Seller ed. — *Immigrant Women* (Temple University Press, 1981).
2. A.V. Arakeri, *Tibetan in India: The Uprooted People and Their Cultural Transplantation* (Reliance Publishing House, New Delhi,) 1998.
3. *Ibid.*
4. *Tibetan Women: Oppression and Discrimination in Occupied Tibet* — (National Report on Tibetan Women, issued by the Tibetan Administration in Dharamshala, India for the Fourth World Conference on Women, Beijing, 1995).
5. *Ibid*
6. *op. cit. 2.*
7. (1) Tibetan Women, (2) Tibetan Women Today (3) Women of Tibet (China Intercontinental Press) and (4) my interviews conversations etc. with hundreds of Tibetan women of all ages and occupation.
8. K. Booth & M. Tienda, *Migration, Gender and Social Change: A Review and Reformulation* (Paper presented at

a UN Conference on this theme at Oslo in June, 1998).

9. *op. cit.* 7.

10. A.C.Bouquet, *Sacred Books of the World* (Cassel London, 1998).

11. *Political Persecution and Human Rights Abuses Against Tibetan Women* (Tibetan Women's Association & Youth Congress, 1998).

12. *op. cit.* 7.

7

Gender-Equal Society As a Model (The Tibetan Women in Exile)

However much the Tibetans may feel nostalgic about their pre-"Chinese occupation" society in Tibet, the Tibetan Women's Association, in its Report to the Fourth World Conference on Women (at Beijing), could not deny the fact that "before the Chinese occupation, the position of women in Tibet was not one of equality...There has been some improvement in the relative position of women in Tibet in the past forty years; but progress has been much slower than elsewhere in the world, and definitely much slower than with the Tibetan community in exile." The Report also admits that "traditionally girls in Tibet had fewer educational opportunities." In exile the girls are more educated than the boys. (This trend is found in all societies if the girls get equal opportunities). On an average, for every 100 male graduates there were 117 female graduates (in the 1990s). Girls outnumber boys even in vocational training courses, viz: 231: 217. It is worth mentioning here that this society has the unique distinction of having a favourable gender ratio for women. It is 51: 49 in Tibetan Autonomous Region. A comprehensive census of the Tibetans in exile has not yet been attempted.

The said Report also admits that there was feudalism in pre-1951 Tibet. But it attempts to justify by pointing out that "all the great nations of today went through periods of feudalism, slavery, casteism and other medieval evils". It can also be taken as a confession that the social system in Tibet was "evil". Was it an admission that the People's Republic of China's "action" in Tibet contributed to the "liberation of a nation which endured in backwardness even in this modern age"? The top spiritual-cum-temporal leader of this nation, His Holiness the Dalai Lama also says that the "traditional Tibetan society was, by no means, perfect; it was in need of changes." Those changes were sincerely initiated and is in the process of continuous implementation ever since the Tibetan government-in-exile started functioning. But, "it was not as bad as China wants the world to believe", adds the leader. He makes a very valid point that reforms got to come from within; that is how it happens and has always happened in all other societies and "no country can be allowed to invade, occupy, annex and colonize another country just because the latter's social structure does not please the former!"[1]

There can be no second opinion about the moral and political validity of this statement. Any external aggression or occupation definitely is a grave violation of human rights. But, a researcher like me, fighting untiringly and uncompromisingly for women's rights (in other words, gender equality), faces an almost irresolvable dilemma. Having seen such a fast change towards equality, particularly gender equality, I cannot but wonder if the Chinese "occupation" was a necessary evil or a blessing in disguise ! Power, in whatever form or from whatever source, is anti-equality and, therefore, anti-people. Power structure builds up and survives on division, discrimination and gross injustice. There is an inherent structure of gender oppression even in a society which gives power to the people. What, then, the women should do in such a situation?...[2] Neither the Tibetan women nor the initiators of gender equality in this society in exile are able to say if this society would have changed so beautifully if feudalism continued or this society did not get the rude jolt from the external aggression.

The Tibetan women in exile (in India)-even the old ladies, who had spent the major part of their lives without freedom and justice-cannot, now, think of a life without these. They feel sorry for the local Indian women around; they do not also understand how "democracy" in India is so much lagging behind, (being 10 years ahead of theirs). These women from the Darjeeling district (where this community has been living since many generations before 1959) find it difficult to believe and accept that their society in their homeland was so backward and unjust. The educated among them do accept this fact because their academic training do not allow them to reject truth or hard facts. But they undergo a terrible inner struggle trying to adjust to this fact. The Women's Associations try to explain this uncomfortable fact by digging out some kind of history from the 2nd. century A.D. In the annals of Suishu and T'ang shu Sui and of the T'ang dynasty there is a reference to the existence of a women's kingdom in south-eastern Tibet. That society, therefore, must have been matriarchal and matrilineal. This report further states, "political power appeared to have been in the hands of women....The mothers of the emperors in the period 7th. to 9th. cent. A.D. are believed to have played active roles in the polity of the state." The words "appeared" and "believed" are carefully chosen; we must place our careful attention to the meanings & implications of these words while attempting to judge the acceptability of such claims. The Report goes on to give inspiring examples of brave warriors and shrewd administrators from among women-particularly of those who resisted the Chinese aggression and got killed.

The Report talks of a mixed economy of agriculture, animal husbandry & trade and women's involvement in all these activities; it even portrays them as major partners in decision-making. The Report also claims that the division of labour was more complementary than exploitative, thereby trying to establish that there was equality even in feudal Tibet. It further claims that there was "a tendency towards social and economic equality and there was no gender division of labour."[3] Such grossly incorrect statements, I am afraid, betrays the antecedents of the "important" members of the association, who,like in any other feudal or bourgeois society, belong to the educated upper class, donning the confidence to assert and influence. They, therefore, become the natural leaders. They very well, may have belonged to the feudal or the aristocratic class in pre-1951 Tibet. The society here is so class-equal that it is not possible to ascertain anybody's class ancestry. In PRC-occupied Tibet,on the other hand, the women who have risen or made some mark are invariably from the peasant, deprived /disabled and lower classes. The following are a few examples.

Ms.Tsering Dolkar, Vice-President of the People,s Government of the TAR, was a serf before "liberation". She was an orphan because her mother died due to absence of any medical benefits for the poor and,therefore, Ms. Dolkar worked as a "maid" in the household of a tribal Chief when she was only 7-13 years old. Needless to add, she was often beaten for not being able to perform perfectly. Many people say that Ms. Dolkar was the founder of modern Tibet's health service and they feel that "the work she has done is like the stars in the sky—visible but uncountable."[4]

Ms.Pasang, whose parents were slaves, held the post before Ms. Dolkar. Her mother died in an epidemic when Pasang was only eight and hereditarily occupied the position of a slave. She was sold to another "lord" when she was twelve. She recounts in her memoirs that there used to be "free" people in the PLA farms opposite her village. She used to envy them. That started giving her confidence and courage to fight and finally, one day, in 1956, she gathered the courage to run away. She signed up for work and joined a school. In 1971, she became the Secretary of the Communist Party of the TAR. She has participated in many policy making meetings. There are 40 Tibetan women in the People's Govt. as Directors of departments and bureaus.

Ms. Tsering Lhamo, who also was a hereditary slave, organised the emancipated serfs to set up the first productive mutual aid team in Tibet. Thus, she became a labour model, a deputy to the Autonomous Region's People's Congress and Vice-Director to the Revolutionary Committee of the TAR. She, thus, became a household name.[5]

There are quite a few assertions, as well, about women's freedom & equality in feudal Tibet. There was no way to find out if those were actually true or not. The available recorded history does not talk of women particularly...it talks of the people in general. It has been generally found in case of histories of the other civilizations / nations that the accepted, expected, run-of-the-mill happenings or features do not find any mention. From the silence of the history-writers of Tibet & China it can, perhaps, be assumed that the position of the women and the serfs in feudal Tibet was as expected or as found in all other similar societies.

On the other hand, our inquiry into the possible causes behind the amazingly egalitarian society in exile can become easier if we believe in what the women freedom fighters are claiming about the position of women in pre-democratic Tibet. The Report starts by claiming that

1. Women were engaged in agriculture & trade and had a "major" share in the decision making.

2. Polyandry was as common as polygamy, depending on the specific economic situation of that area or that population and their consequent needs. But, as everybody knows, the present "modern" society in exile has automatically accepted monogamy only as a necessary modern norm. The transition and its acceptance have been marvelously fast and smooth, without the slightest resistance, discomfort or unhappiness. In fact, both men and women, young and old are very happy and grateful to their govt. and the Indian govt. Amazingly, again, men are so relaxed and comfortable with the changes which have transferred their age-old power phenomenally to their counterparts. This is the reason why this society, in its present form, can be and should be taken as a model for our society (or, for any other gender-unequal society).

3. Divorce and re-marriage,including widow re-marriage, were acceptable. This sounds more a "claim" than truth, because divorce is not encouraged even in the present gender-equal society. The present "modern" society puts lot of sanctity to the family bonds and to the duties of each member of a family towards each other, particularly to the great emotional support that each member can give and needs to give to the other and to all others. Accordingly, this society discourages divorce or any other "unsettling" happening, and encourages serious couselling with sincere perseverance—quite similar to the commune system in PRC. There are government-employed counsellors and social workers in PRC to do this

job. Thus, one can assume that similar pro-people/ pro-women measures must have been implemented in the Tibetan Autonomous Region also.

But the society in exile is a better model because this equality has come naturally, without being imposed from an authority. Such a model, therefore, can inspire and "goad", without any coercion.

Widow marriage is highly encouraged in the present society—due to the same reason of emphasis on solidarity and sanctity of the family. They do not believe in male superiority, though they believe that a father-figure is necessary for the psychological and emotional support of the family members, particularly the children.

4. Arranged marriage was the norm, the bride moving over to her husband's family after her marriage. But, a female child, if she is the only child, could, and usually did, live with her parents even after her marriage. Married girls live with their parents if the latter are alone or are not looked after by their other /male children. Such customs are born out of their superiormost concern for and obligations towards their parents and the aged.

   At the same time, they do not allow the aged to feel that they are a liability. The" grandparents"- however old and infirm—are "employed" in the handicrafts centres, and whatever little they can contribute to the economy is "extracted" out of them. No pity, but lots of concern, is shown to them. Thus, unlike in our or in any bourgeois society, nobody—whatever the age or the sex—feels neglected, rejected /deprived. Not pitied, but cared.

5. The real revolutionary aspect of their feudal society before 1951 seems to be the right of not to get

> married. This is inconceivable for anybody (man or woman), trained in the powerful patriarchal ideology. In any such society, the woman does not belong to herself—not even her body, nor her social identity. She is merely a machine for production, reproduction and the carnal pleasures of her male counterpart. So, no society allows its women to remain unmarried or, in other words, independent of the male control. In the Tibetan society, an unmarried girl is rather at an advantage. She does not face the problem of being controlled by her in-laws and/or husband, and not even by her father!

This society puts good value to celibacy and spiritual life. The families pay much respect to the nuns and, they feel happy and honoured about their children becoming nuns and monks. The women consider it a "great honour and grace" to be the mother of the Dalai Lamas, the Panchen Lamas, the Rinpoches or even of the ordinary monks and nuns. In the post-migration era the nuns are held in high esteem also because of their valiant struggle for the liberation of their land.

B

Let us, now, look at the other side of the picture. The consciousness about their right over their body is complete among the women. They demand the freedom of not having children, of not getting married or of having as many children as they desire. For them both sex and motherhood should be totally and exclusively according to their own desires and pleasures. "Tibetan women, like women all over the world, should have the inalienable right to control their bodies and their right to privacy should be protected," writes the Report to the Fourth World Conference while condemning the "atrocities" in China-occupied Tibet. ...Little do they know that the "right to body & privacy" is not at all the right of any woman anywhere -else in the world. It is there only in their own society under the new government in exile.

This protest was lodged because of the PRC law in TAR (Tibetan Autonomous Region) due to which more than two children per couple is not allowed. They, in their zest for protest against PRC rule, ignore two very important facts. First, this PRC law has been relaxed for Tibetan nationals in deference to the Tibetan traditions. The ruling ethnic group or the Han Chinese are allowed only one child (notwithstanding the tradition and belief, amongst them also, of having as many children as the Creator or Nature wants). Secondly, the Tibetans in exile or the free Tibetans themselves, are voluntarily going for small families. (i) Economic freedom and prosperity, (ii) the accompanying ambition & desire for a better life and (iii) exposure to the secular, liberal & consumerist values have given their mind the kind of thinking and training which a thousand-and-a-one family planning programmes (in the deeply rooted patriarchal society like India) could not achieve.

Another curious thing about the psyche of the women in exile, dedicated to the cause of their homeland's liberation, is that while decrying the PRC measures for family planning, they are demanding "social support systems for health, *family planning* and education"! By this, they are demanding first, the exclusive right over their own body & sexuality, which, in other words, is their right to privacy / individuality & identity. The last is the most vital right for any human person, without which he/ she is merely a human body, and not a human person. Secondly, they are exercising their experiential knowledge that limited resources can feed only limited number of mouths. Women excel in this kind of knowledge, and that is why in all fields, including environment management & developmental planning, their inputs are useful and practical. The nation strongly believes in complete political independence and sovereignty over its own affairs. It abhors begging and borrowing. Rightly, they have blamed the absence of a social support system for health, family planning & education as the cause of poverty which, in turn, "exposes women to extreme hardship in gaining employment & educational opportunities." It appears that these half- educated Tibetan women or activists are echoing the doyen of Welfare Economics, Nobel Laureate Prof. Amartya Sen!

Interestingly, the Tibetan women activists do not consider "women's experience of poverty" more oppressive, but only different (from that of men's). This is amply indicative of the absence of gender- based exploitation & discrimination which forces a woman to become anti-male. Freedom, particularly economic freedom, is a part & parcel of their culture and mental training. Yet, they think "as long as China controls Tibetan economy, Tibetan women will not be able to participate in the economic decision-making processes that affect their future lives."

C

The vast opening to modern, secular education, both in Tibetan Autonomous Region and in exile has done the trick. Though they are extremely grateful to the Indian government for opening Tibetan Central Schools and thus, giving them very good opportunities for education, they show extreme resentment to similar endeavours by the Chinese government in TAR. The commoners and women were totally denied education in pre-1951 Tibet. The present Tibetans realise fully well the progressive and civilisational benefits from the secular and scientific educational agenda; they perceive the marvelous transformation in their life and thinking that education can bring; yet they lament the "loss of religious freedom" for the monks and nuns in TAR. A video film, shot at Lhasa and a few other places of TAR by an Indian, shows the ecclesiastical and lay Tibetans *freely* performing their religious rites; it also shows the Potala palace and a few monasteries getting a facelift or getting renovated. People's Republic of China has openly apologised for the excesses committed during the Cultural Revolution. The Han Chinese also have suffered immensely due to that. The Tibetans should try to understand, in their own good, that the "excesses" of the notorious Cultural Revolution were not merely against them or other cultural minorities. People's Republic of China is now trying its best to undo, restore and renovate.

The Report also laments the absence of the opportunities in TAR for learning their own language. But, the afore-mentioned video clearly shows hoardings of schools, training centres, shops, hospitals, etc. written in Tibetan language and script (and, at places, in Mandarin), thereby unambiguously indicating the equal, if not higher, importance of the Tibetan language in Tibet. I have also met Han Chinese who have taken special care to learn the language of the people because they desire to work in the TAR. If the Tibetan language had no place of importance in China-occupied Tibet, why should the Chinese then feel the necessity to learn that language?

The monasteries and the nunneries are now being meticulously renovated. ... I may sound anti-national, but I cannot help pointing out that one experiences religious coercion in 'secular' India, a complete freedom to practice or not to practice any religion in a communist or areligious China! Lately, the Peoples' Republic of China is rather keen for a dialogue or even third-party intervention.The wise and pragmatic leader of the Tibetans, the present Dalai Lama, is expressing equal amount of eagerness for cooperation. But the refugees are not very happy with their leader in this matter, though the Indian-Tibetans, (that is, those who are living in India for many generations,) are not much bothered about it. They are more bothered about India and about what happens to India, about India's foreign policies and other countries' policies towards India. They are not much aware of the "oppressions" by the Communist government of China since they were born and brought up in India and do not know much about the Tibetan society in Tibet; nor do they know much about PRC or its international politics. They lend their voice, in a sense of unity, for a "free" Tibet. But unity and fraternity are their only concern. They are not so passionate about freedom.

The Tibetans' chief objection to Mandarin is that it is a foreign language. But, strangely, they do not feel the same about English which is the medium of instruction in all Tibetan Central Schools in India! On the contrary, they are very happy about the easy and universal access to English language and modern secular education in exile. The feudal lords used to regularly send their children (girls were not excluded) to Darjeeling for English language and secular studies because there was no provision for such in their own land. These feudal lords even had a limited family. The modern Tibetans talk of cultural values that do not permit them to "go against Nature", or what happens "naturally"(in reference to family planning). The Report also points out "while the Chinese in Tibet study English right from the primary school stage, Tibetans are taught this language only when they reach the third year at Upper Middle School level."

My experience with the young Tibetans, who keep migrating and freely moving across the international border every now & then is very different. (This freedom of movement is itself indicative of a non- oppressive government in TAR). All of them are as conversant in English as they are with their mother tongue. In fact, majority of them do not know Chinese at all. Yet, the Report writes "the medium of teaching from Middle School level upwards is Chinese." Besides, if Chinese is taught only from *upper* middle school level, then what is the language of teaching at the levels lower than the middle school? Obviously nothing else but Tibetan, because the Report also complains that the opportunities to learn English is limited.

The Report, further says that education in Tibet is "neither free nor universally available" and that "an overwhelming number of Tibetan girls still do not go to school because either there are no schools or the parents cannot afford". But this is factually incorrect not only from their own reporting (in other pages of the same report), but from the conversations with the young girls who have migrated or traveled to India recently (much after 1959). Secondly, the Report talks of the benefits of modern universal education (even if it is not in Tibetan language) on the one hand, but of the lost benefits of teachings in the monasteries and nunneries (over 6259 in number) on the other! Contradicting their own observations elsewhere (in the report) and in sundry other reports and statements (while expressing their deep gratitude to the Govt. of India), they claim that these monasteries and nunneries "served as schools & universities, fulfilling Tibet's unique educational needs. Drepung monastery in Lhasa alone had, at any given time, over 10,000 students coming mostly from the peasantry. In addition, there was a sizable network of private & government schools all over Tibet."...Such statements are contradicting the statements of His Holiness even!

Next, the Report talks of (i) only urban-based health service,and (ii) only 2 doctors per 1,000 in rural areas (in China-occupied Tibet) - as if the situation is any better in India or in any other developing country. The Report does not even talk highly about the amenities available to them in India. It also blames the "overall low level of health awareness in the community". Besides, why do they need modern doctors at all if everything traditional and everything pre-1951 was so good and so beneficial? The Tibetans have such a wonderful medicine system with which they are doing miracles in India and even in highly developed countries. This system succeeds where Allopathy and Homeopathy fail.

The Report rightly concludes "while women all over the world suffer discrimination, violence and other violations, the struggle they are voicing is largely for women's liberation. Tibet's own struggle embodies another element viz; national survival, reversal of genocide & the fight to return to our own occupied homeland....Tibetan refugee women have had to adapt to a new way of life and, at the same time, struggle to maintain our culture and identity".

D

According to the Tibetans, who are settled in India for many generations, have got Indian citizenship and consider themselves Indians, the Tibetan society, which was not gender-equal in Tibet, has become so in exile (or in India) because of the following reasons:-

1. exposure to democratic atmosphere all over the world,
2. exposure to democratic norms in India, (though, in reality, the Indian society has miles to go before it can claim to have reached that goal),
3. the democratic nature of Dalai Lama, and consequently
4. intent and content of their democratic Constitution.

The following are the clear indicators of gender equality in the Tibetan society in exile.

1. The *Sex Ratio* is female friendly, viz: 52:48. There are absolutely no instance of female foeticide or infanticide. The baby girls get as much of care and nutrition as the baby boys. The mother0 too, be she of a boy or of a girl, gets as much care and nutrition as the family can afford. Being a communitarian and egalitarian society, the new mother and the new baby may get all the help (in whichever way) from the members of the community, particularly of the neighbourhood.

2. There is no preference for a male child and no humiliation of the mother for not having produced a male child. Motherhood is extremely precious and, like in India, is considered a woman's greatest virtue. But, unlike in India,they are sincere about what they profess and believe in. In India women are addressed as 'mothers' to be burdened with responsibilities only—with no rights and privileges. They are abused, tortured, humiliated and even raped.

   There is, therefore, no notion of an "illegitimate" child (in the Tibetan society) and a single mother—widow, divorced or unmarried—is at no disadvantage; nor is she censored or humiliated. Seldom does it happen that the father of the child denies responsibility. Neglect of a mother or a child can never be tolerated by the community, society or the administration.

3. *Sexual Abuse* or the violation of the woman's body is so very non-existent in the society of the exiles that even the activist women of the Tibetan Women's Association find it difficult to understand its magnitude and ugliness. They have a theoretical knowledge, gathered from the numerous reportings in the Indian newspapers and from their conversations with their Indian friends and

neighbours. Interestingly, Indian men do not "dare" to misbehave with the Tibetan girls of their locality, though the latter are usually ,like the hill & tribal girls in general, uninhibited and unsuspecting.

The reasons behind the absence of sexual abuse may be two.

(i) Sex is not a taboo and the scciety does not condemn free mixing before marriage provided, of course, that both are mature enough and behave responsibly with each other, for the sake of their own future. What is really important is that a man is held as responsible as a woman is for the consequences. In India only the raped woman or the unmarried mother is condemned and ostracised. The culprit moves about freely.

(ii) marriage is held as a noble institution; it is considered sacred and eternally binding. Extra-marital relations or sex is not accepted. But, instead of condemning, prolonged and serious counseling is done by friends, relatives, neighbours and official counselors. With all their efforts, sincerity and perseverance, they try their utmost to stop a marriage from breaking. To them a mother and her children are of highest importance. I would say that this deeply rooted strong belief, (which has the fervour of a religious belief), has made this society so very gender sensitive and gender equal. The root-cause of gender-inequality lies, to my mind, in the unabashed violation of the woman's body, her reproductivite ability and sexuality. In patriarchal societies a woman's productivity and reproductivity are the property of men, who deny her the right to any property, including her own.

4. A Tibetan woman cannot, in any case, be denied of any property because customarily property is

not owned by any individual (neither a man nor a woman); it is necessarily owned by a family. Similarly, *all decisions*, whether related to property, children, education, vocation, occupation or the future of the children or of any other member of the family *are taken jontly* by all the mature members of the family including, children who are grown up enough to think and give an opinion. And, a family usually comprises of three generations (may be even four)—they have so much of respect and concern for the old and their seniors.

This cultural trait is found very much in our "adivasi" societies also. They still retain the humane values of a human society. Interestingly,the modern Chinese society of the Communist regime continues to value such humane feelings and duties. Both the Chinese and the Tibetan societies have imbibed only the *valuable* aspects of the "modern" values from the West, while retaining the values of their own traditions.(In India, unfortunately, only Western vices, viz: consumerism, is copied; respect for traditional values is superficial and insincere).

A Tibetan woman in exile is totally independent economically; she is more into business and trade; she comfortably moves around—far & near—with her woollens & other merchandise; she is also into restaurant management and shop-keeping...A woman earning more than her husband or running the house with her single income does not bring any shame or social stigma to the man or to the family; nor is her income grabbed by her husband or other patriarchs. Whoever may be the earner, *the income is family's* and the family's only, and the family as a whole /collectively takes the decision regarding its spending. Young, school going children also have a say.

But, we must not forget that the situation was not so golden for the women and children in feudal Tibet. The socio-economic situation was more or less the same as it used to be in any other feudal society. The feudal lords used to be as authoritarian and assertive as they were expected to be by the virtue of their position of power. This attitude was displayed not only to their serfs but also towards their own women, who were forced to remain indoors and not be part of any productive work. So women could not have been involved in any decision making or owning of the family property.

Being totally confined to the four walls of their household and worklessness, the Tibetan women of the feudal days must have also been devoid of any freedom. Therefore,they must have also run the risk of being sexually abused by their husbands (in case of the Nobles' wives) and by their landlords (in case of the serfs' wives). There are no clear accounts about this.

5. Related to this is the very important aspect of dowry—the real doom in a woman's life in South Asia. The question does not arise at all in a situation where women are not bought and sold, where women are not property but are themselves, owners of property. A *dowryless* society and a society where women and children have equal property rights is not only gender-equal, but also egalitarian from every aspect.For example, in the hills of Himachal Pradesh in India,and may be with so many other "original inhabitants" (the adivasis) of India, the "dowry" is given collectively by the community or the "biradari"(nearest translation of which is "brotherhood"). The newly married do need a few basic things to start their 'new life together' comfortably and without hardship. Property, if owned collectively and for

the benefit of the "collective" /community /society, is necessary, and even developmental. Then it becomes not only by the people and of the people, but also *for* the people. *Such* property builds a nation, does not divide. Absence of individual and selfish ownership of property frees a society of bondages and bindings. In such a situation there are no owners or owned and, therefore, no divisions or inequalities in the society.

6. Like in most societies, the Tibetan women, in general, shift to their husbands' homes after marriage. But it is not an inalterable practice. A married woman is advised to stay with her old parents if she is their only child or if her siblings are not in a position to do their duties to their parents. Besides, as pointed out several times earlier, she does not lose her individuality or independence by attaining the status of a married woman. She does not need to change her surname .... Actually, there are no surnames or family names among the Tibetans. Every individual, man or woman, has an individual /exclusive name of his /her own, which neither shows his /her family nor the person's sex. All Tibetan names are unisexual,— I have met so many girls called Tenzin and so many boys of the same name!

This is true of every other name. Interestingly,this is so with the Chinese names also. This cultural practice is very important for the liberation of any group "bonded" by their deprivation. True, human beings need to come together, form a group and work co-operatively for his /her individual benefit along with the group's or the community's and, therefore, a human society is unavoidable and inevitable. But, at the same time, individuality or an individual's freedom is as important and necessary for human civilization to go ahead, progress and prosper. An individual, should be free to be in and out of a group or a society at his /her own free will and should not be bound down by an identity imposed on it by the society or the societal norms and practices. Absence of surnames and gender-specific names clearly indicate the absence of strict and clear-cut divisions on the basis of sex, caste and parentage/ family identity.

The naming system in India turns an individual into 'a statement by the society,' he /she is known by her caste, religion and sex and also by her marital status in case of a woman. The individual is, thus, "fated" from before its birth and even after death! The treatment and the opportunities that he /she gets from the society, or even from the State, is pre-determined and irrevocable and according to his /her socio-religious position. Very few can break this shackle and come out as an "individual". Even if, in a few cases, the opportunities are equal and there are no apparent discriminations, the barrier created by the "identity of surname" cannot really be broken or ignored totally. The identity of marital status and the caste makes it much more difficult for a woman. Thus, it is an extremely significant indicator of a Tibetan woman's equality and freedom.

E

Let us, now,inquire into the long and short details of a Tibetan woman's life and status in the present society (i.e. in exile). As mentioned earlier the present study is based heavily on my day-to-day interactions and prolonged casual conversations with the women from various walks of life in various northern Indian settlements. Structured questionnaires were used to interview teachers, students, professionals, govt. officials, etc. but, the real feel of the situation could be got from the friendly, casual chit chats only. By nature they are friendly, uninhibited and forthcoming. They are warm and hospitable to those whom they regard as their friends. They are totally "natural" and—if they speak they speak the truth only; if they do not want to come out openly, they will rather not speak. They just cannot weigh their words or be diplomatic. This is universally true about all — men, women, highly or less educated, highly placed govt. official or an ordinary shopkeeper.

1. Though both polygamy and polyandry—depending on the social position and the economic need of a family—were quite common in feudal Tibet and, therefore, marriages were necessarily arranged, the present society is totally monogamous and the partners are mostly out of free choice. Dowry is still not in vogue and the family property continues to be family property only, with no individual ownership or patriarchal decision-taking whatsoever. As a necessary corollary to this, the wife or the daughter-in-law is not deprived, ill-treated, tortured or killed. Marital disputes are also minimal. In any capitalist situation a majority of the disputes and violence in any relationship — be it husband & wife, brothers & sisters, parents & children, friends or partners—originate from property or proprietorship.

   The other reasons for disputes are also almost absent as those are usually born out of discriminations, humiliations and grotesquely unequal treatments. Yet, when divorces are sought due to the personal nature of a partner or due to one of them falling in love with somebody else, prolonged and persistent counseling is done by the community as well as by the government welfare officers. Marriage and motherhood are regarded sacred and, therefore, highest value is attached to the rights of a mother and her children.

   A family earns for (i) its children (or, rather, the

"future generation" of the nation), (ii) the nation and its freedom and (iii) the family monastery. The Tibetans in India keep a minimum of 10% of their family income earmarked for their freedom struggle and their family lama or monastery. They also have the notions of normal profit and extra profit. A hotel-owner or a shopkeeper for example, gives away the 'excess' income earned, may be, due to tourist rush or any other reason. Like the hill people or the adivasis, the Tibetans are very fond of good living, fun and enjoyment, but they do not want one rupee more than what they need. They have voluntarily drawn a line of their contentment and they seldom transgress that. The capitalist world and the mainstream Indians do not believe in drawing the Lakshman Rekha of contentment for themselves and thus, they are never happy with however much they get or earn (though their religions talk of austerity and sacrifices).

2. There is no notion of individual ownership of money or property. Everything belongs to and is decided by the family as a unit. The children too, have an equal say and of course, the opinions of the old parents are held in great regard. There is no taboo about that 'men only should earn and that a man should not be economically dependent on his wife'. It is not a matter of shame if the husband is not earning or is not able to earn. Interestingly, the women are more active in every field including economic. We have seen the fearless and determined role of the nuns in their fight against the Chinese oppression (political).

3. Since the men /husbands do not feel ashamed of living on wife's earning, they do not also feel shy or ashamed of engaging themselves in all household activities including taking care of their children

and infants. An unemployed husband or son does all that a woman or a housewife does in a patriarchal society. In case of both being employed or engaged in business, the household work and the care of the aged and the young are shared according to the workload or the convenience of each adult individual in the family.

The old are respected and lovingly taken care of, but they are encouraged to work as much as they can. They are neither expected nor allowed to sit idle the whole day. Adequate care is taken, both by the government and the family, to ensure that the elderly do not feel redundant or neglected. They are made to remain economically "useful", so that they never feel unwanted or depressed. In the Handicrafts Centres for example, the oldest of the old are given some work and made to earn. But there is no coercion or strictness. Whatever little they produce is happily accepted and acknowledged. There are no old age homes, because a normal Tibetan family comprises of three to four generations with every single member—whatever may be his /her age or economic capability—having a say in the affairs of the family.

4. Since unlike in any other society, unlike even in the most egalitarian of the tribal societies, the children have an equal role in decision making, child abuse of any kind or degree is totally inconceivable in this society. It is necessary to repeat at this point that there is also no concept of an "illegitimate" child or of a woman "ashamed" of being an unwed mother, notwithstanding the fact that immense sanctity is attached to the institution of marriage. Generally, children do not also have to suffer as "orphans", because widow marriage is highly encouraged and

a father figure is considered greatly desirable for a healthy family and for the normal growth of a child. A society or a community, which gives the right kind of respect and recognition to women and children, cannot but be egalitarian and therefore, a model for others. They are the most vulnerable in any other society because they are the easiest targets and victims of patriarchy.

5. As mentioned several times before, such an egalitarian society has become possible because of the absence of individual ownership of property. Anybody believing in human rights as the basic and the ultimate rights for any human being cannot deny the truth that greed and selfishness born out of individual ownership and therefore, accumulation are at the root of all deprivation, discrimination and oppression (whichever part of the world or whichever socio-economic stratum the person may be from). He /she also knows that the unending and ever-increasing lust for accumulation by usurping others'legitimate share is the birthplace of capitalism. Patriarchy was born out of capitalism and religion and the fear of God was created to justify this kind of robbing and the depriving. Women,thus, got robbed of their opportunities to education and earning and of the recognition of their capabilities. Caste system in India was created with the same motive. Judging from this angle, it appears that migration and the consequent dispossession from land and property of the upper class Tibetans have turned out to be a boon in disguise for the community.This kind of egalitarianism could not have been possible in pre-migration feudal Tibet and particularly, where power was concentrated in the hands of the ecclesiastical community.

6. The establishment of the Tibetan Central Schools

(by the Govt. of India) and the Tibetans' eagerness for learning, so that they can get well-settled in life, have strengthened the egalitarianism in their society. It has been a dramatic change from almost total illiteracy to total literacy and higher education. The education system in pre-modern Tibet was only for the lamas and only the children of a few feudal lords were lucky enough to get modern secular education from the Christian missionary schools in Darjeeling, India. Educational opportunities are not all that inadequate for the Indians either. There is "universal" education for all Indians, according to the Constitution . But the majority of the Indians continue to remain uneducated and even far from mere literacy because the Constitutional Directive to make education compulsory has not been implemented in the 49 long years. The Tibetans in exile has made education compulsory for themselves willingly, without any external pressure of Constitutional directive or governmental law.

These schools are also the centres for the learning of their dances, songs, etc. and the development of their culture. Patriotism or the love for their own land and environment— both Natural and cultural—is also instilled in the heart and mind of the young Tibetans for whom their present settlement, India and everything Indian is a reality and their true life. Tibet is a dream and the love for Tibet is a taught sentiment. They are all born and brought up in India, in an overwhelmingly Indian atmosphere; their parents too, are Indians (in a majority of cases). For them Tibet and its "desecration" in the hands of the Chinese "imperialists" is merely a story told by their grandparents or the activists who try to inspire them into patriotism.

I met students—quite a few of them—who do not know for sure why they must leave their "birthplace" (viz:India),where they are happy and face no problems at all. No other refugees have been treated so cordially and given so many benefits as this community has been. They are told by the activists about the greatness of one's motherland and one's love for it. They are also repeatedly told that they are mere refugees in this country and that is a status of disgrace. So, the only motto in their life and work should be to join in the nation's struggle for freedom and ultimately go back to their *own* land. Almost all of them come out with this "taught" answer but, they become silent and uncomfortable when asked to explain in what respect free Tibet will be better than India and what are the problems they are now facing in exile. The only answer they have is 'this is exile, they are refugees here and every human being, with a sense of dignity,likes to live in one's own country'. ...Some of the girls were so frank that they expressed their strong desire not to leave India.

The Tibetans in the Darjeeling district felt and claimed that they are Indians only; they did not like to be referred to as refugees. They have voting rights and a majority of the men are serving in the Indian defence services. They feel disturbed when PRC has an aggressive posture towards India: they have nothing much to say about China's aggression in Tibet. Some of them are the middle-aged women, who may have migrated as toddlers and did not encounter the Chinese "barbarism" directly. They whispered into my ears that they did not understand this "extra- territorial" sentiment of the Tibetans. They also confessed that they do not have the courage to question these "patriots"(meaning those Tibetans who are clamouring to return to Tibet) but they do not have any sympathy for their "cause".

These non-refugee Tibetans have got nicely assimilated with the local Indians comprising of the Nepalese, Sikkimese, Marwari traders and shopkeepers and a few Bengalis (who are mostly the bureaucrats and the professionals). All of them speak the Nepali language (the lingua franca of that region), eat "dal" and vegetables cooked in the Nepali or the Bengali styles and are not particular about interacting with the Tibetans *only* (unlike those in the settlements like Dharamshala, Shimla, Delhi and Calcutta). The college-going girls may have more Nepali friends than Tibetan. It is important to note here that the Nepalese themselves originally are migrants like the Tibetans but now, all of them are Indian citizens and consider themselves Indians only. Therein lies the greatness of our great land and culture. It is a beautiful "bouquet" civilization, where nobody knows for sure who or which group is originally Indian or not. All Indians, including the Aryans, are migrants only. The 'recent' migrants are usually taken as foreigners or refugees, depending on the motive or the reason behind their migration. No clear-cut time frame is attached to the concept of this "recent". The Tibetans of the Darjeeling district, for example, are not considered refugees, neither by themselves nor by the local residents.

There are two major aspects in which the Indian-Tibetans have retained their uniqueness, viz:the women's dress and their religious faith and practice. They are not very happy about marriage outside their religion because they feel that the "outsider" will face tremendous adjustment problems. I must say that they are very pragmatic because religion-cum-culture or religion-based culture is a community's most deep rooted sentiment and the worst adjustment or acceptance problems crop out of that. They do not believe in forced or helpless conversions due to inter-religious marriages because they believe that religious faith and cultural practices are rooted, natural and therefore, voluntary. Notwithstanding such beliefs and reservations, the Tibetans are not fanatical against inter-cultural nuptial knots. Marriages with the Sikkimese and the Buddhist Nepalese are not uncommon. I have met a few who have even married Hindu Indians, who have not been made to give up their religious practice and have their very private "Pooja" rooms/ corners.

The problem is quite pronounced in the refugee settlements because the local population around are non-Buddhists and they have quite a bit of reservations about these settlers. They have a grudge that these "foreigners" have been allowed to grab their lands and eat up the "scarce" resources of "poor" India. It may not be too irrelevant to add here that this "foreigner" phoebia is pronounced only among the Indians belonging to the mainstream culture; to them every non-Aryan in India is an intruder and an alien.

7. A real enigma to me was the possible rationale behind the formation of Tibetan Women's Associations in each and every settlement! Usually women's associations are formed or women come together in order to fight male oppression or the suffocating hold of patriarchy. This is the practice all over the world including the developed countries. Economic development or prosperity need not necessarily liberate the women and the other minorities. The Tibetan women in exile have formed the associations to strengthen themselves not against male oppression (because that hardly

ever exists). They seek to strengthen themselves through unity, for the liberation of their occupied land. Rapes, dowries, tortures, killings are no issues for them at all. They talk of tortures and killings by the Chinese soldiers. Tortures by the in-laws and other patriarchal and caste autocrats which their Indian and other South Asian counterparts suffer daily, every minute of their existence, are mere concepts to them. They know about these kinds of oppressions and dehumanisation through their exposures to the Indian films, newspapers and the society around. They get horrified and fail to understand why it is so! These are as much an enigma for them as the absence of these in their society is an enigma for me.

(i) Rapes within the community is zero. It was not so rampant even during feudal cultural structure. Even marital rapes are like zero because of (a) the overall atmosphere of gender equality, (b) the uninhibited attitude towards sex as something pleasurable and desirable, and so why spoil it by force, fear or coercion? and (c) the sacred value attached to the socially important roles of the mother, father and their children....There have been a few attempts at molestation by the local or the tourist Indians, but the girls themselves have shown immense courage and strength. It was noticed, interestingly, that the local males are a bit weary of the Tibetan girls. The girls, when asked, could not think of a reason. But they are very happy about it. At the level of pure friendship they are very free and warm.

(ii) The Tibetan nation traditionally, ever since the days of recorded history, has been quite similar to the civilizations of Harappa and Mohenjodaro —with no trained or organised army and with no agenda for war, violence or imperialism. The credit cannot solely go to Buddhism. Such philosophy and ideology were much more ancient than Buddhism which did not really have to bring the agenda of peace and non-violence in Tibet. Buddhism merely strengthened the existing faith by giving it a well thought out content and direction. It tried to cleanse the Tibetan system of its excesses in supernatural beliefs and superstitions. Buddhism, thus did all that the soil of Tibetan mind /faith wanted it to sow. And Buddhism continued to spread and remain deep-seated here, more than in any other civilization where it had originally been taken to, because it matched perfectly well with the already existing Tibetan beliefs and culture.

Such a national mind can grow if the people have a natural love for Nature and environment, for music, art, for life and all human values that make living smooth, interdependent and worth living. Buddhism is an ethical religion, showing the path to good and moral living, left to the rationality and understanding of an individual member of the society. There are no gods and therefore, no diktats and no authority. The individual's own moral understanding is the authority.

We have to , once again, come back to the point that the total absence of violence in this culture is because there is no craving for property and no notion of *individual* ownership of property. What will they fight for then ? As discussed above, the absence of the sense of property or ownership has not allowed authoritarianism to grow or patriarchy to take hold of the reins. Thus, I repeat. the ground for violence or the violation of natural human rights could not be prepared. Wife-beating or any other kind of violence against women were also inconsistent with the society's belief and behaviour structures /patterns. Once in a while there has been casual slapping or hitting in a fit of anger or under the influence of liquor, but there is never an incident of repeated or consistent beating or humiliation. The deeply rooted and pervading ethos of non-aggression and non-violence makes the offender suffer a sense of shame and even, remorse; the woman or the offended also immediately and spontaneously protests and even hits back—not in revenge, but out of a sense of self-respect and dignity as a human being .... Violence, thus, gets nipped in the bud....In our society male violence against women or the violence of the powerful against the "have not"s get worse and worse and perpetuated because the social structure does not allow the tortured to raise their head or voice. Violence or power unopposed is violence or power encouraged and perpetrated.

(iii) Due to the same reason,i.e. the absence of private property and a general level of contentment, there is no notion of dowry in this society. It was absent even during the days of private male ownership of property under feudalism. There was the custom of gifts by the friends and relatives (as it is now). Thus, another very important reason behind the consolidation of women's unity and the formation of women's associations is missing in this society.

(iv) There definitely was a preference for male children in feudal Tibet, but there was no custom of female infanticide or discrimination against female babies with regard to health and nutrition. Girls were kept illiterate no doubt, but boys too, had no scope for education unless they chose to join the monasteries. That kind of education, in any case, was not comprehensive, nor scientific, nor modern

/secular. Some of the enlightened Nobles sent their children to Darjeeling (India) or even to China for education and girls were not held back. Almost all the sisters and female relatives of the XIIIth. and XIVth. Dalai Lamas got educated in Darjeeling and a majority of the Panchen Lama's female relatives in China (pre and post 1949).

Interestingly, the Dalai and the Panchen Lamas always had the opportunities to learn English and other European Languages and get modern Western education! The other lamas, were deprived of this privilege. Even now, after almost 40 years of democratic governance and with the gates of modern secular education opened to all, the lamas are not exposed to non -ecclesiastical education or any non-Tibetan language.The doctors, who are lamas, need interpreters while dealing with the Indian or non-Tibetan patients....The reason behind the two supreme lamas having access to modern education and international languages may be that they are also the temporal leaders of this community and are responsible for its political & economic affairs. They also have to deal with the Heads of nations and speak effectively in world bodies.

The community in exile is totally free of any preference for male children. May be, secretly they even prefer female offsprings as the women in the present society seem to be more economically active; they seem to be having a better knack for business. This fact is adequately proven by the sex ratio which is fully endorsive of what should happen if Nature is not interfered with, i.e. more women and fewer men. Thus, another potential ground for violence against the female sex is totally non- existent. This perhaps, is the one and the only society (apart from a few tribals in the Himalayan regions of India —both in the west and in the east) where there is no gender discrimination whatsoever.

Absence of gender discrimination has been observed even among the rich upper caste orchardists from the Shimla hills. They give equal care and nutrition to the baby girls. The opportunities for and exposure to education are also equal. Due to climatic reasons the age of puberty is not so low like in the hot plains of India. Therefore, child marriage is also uncommon and the girls get ample opportunities to get higher education and take up jobs. Some of the striking features of this hill society are: milk, for example, is first given to the infants, children and nursing mothers, then to the sick and the old and last to the adult male members. There is also no dowry in these societies and the parents of the bride are not burdened with the financial responsibilities of delivery of the baby and the post-delivery cares. On the contrary, the mother of the expectant mother (daughter-in-law) is invited, with full honour and hospitality, to spend a few months with her daughter so that the new mother feels emotionally comfortable at a time when that kind of comfort is very much necessary for the mental and physical health of both the mother and the new-born. The typical North Indian upper caste custom of giving dowry, once again, to the daughter's in-laws on the occasion of the birth of a child is not in practice. All these are a reality notwithstanding the fact that these societies, viz: the hills of Himachal Pradesh and the Tibetan, are surrounded by the highly patriarchal Punjabi or other caste Hindu societies.

(v) Prostitution, like rape, is another word which they try to comprehend through their exposure to the movies, media and the Indian mainstream society around. They feel totally amazed that men derive pleasure out of sex forced against the partner's wish. To them, sex is for pleasure and pleasure only, and therefore, exclusively voluntary and consensual. That is why, their knowledge and awareness about AIDS & STDs are limited. Extra-marital sex is not all that uncommon (though there is a strong societal disapproval about it), but those are always accompanied by willingness, consent and mutual pleasure.

(vi) The Women's Associations do not also have to fight for maintenance or the custody of the children on behalf of a divorced woman. The reasons have already been mentioned earlier. The government and the Family Welfare Officer sees to it that the spouse earning more helps the one earning less; the amount specified is according to the number of mouths to feed. This institution is found in both PRC & TAR and not in any capitalist polity even if that has the face of democracy and "social welfare". Secondly, there is no conception of the children's "custody". The concept of ownership, in any form or in any relationship, is absent from their minds—be it class, gender or family bonds. The word "custody" smacks of ownership. As mentioned a several times earlier, each and every member of a family—father, mother, grandparents and children—have equal participation in all decision making, and nobody is scared or cowed down—not even the woman or the children. Neither the society nor any judicial authority decides who the children of separated parents would like to stay with....the *children themselves,* decide. One child may choose the mother, another the father.

This is the only known society and polity where the non-adults have equal rights and they are as much an entity.

In our society the Dalits fight against oppression, but their women and children are oppressed by them. Women fight against discrimination and exploitation, but their own children are, more often than not, exploited by them only! And children remain ever exploited and freedomless because physically they are weak and their limbs are not fully grown and strong. `They remain overpowered with fear of the adult, be he father, elder brother, teacher or employer. The Tibetan is the only known society which has given full rights and recognition to the youngest and the oldest equally.

The Tibetan Women's Association, formed in all the settlements, have their locus standi in two major activities they are engaged in. One, to advocate the values and benefits of stable relationships without which there cannot be an overall conflictless and peaceful atmosphere in the family and the society. Counseling is a major duty /role, therefore. The chief aim, as we know, of the Tibetan migrant community, of its government in exile, of all the citizens, and, of the said association is to *unite, remain united and derive unlimited strength through this unity* so that the struggle for country's liberation does not lose its power and momentum. That is why and also for various other humane reasons (discussed on several occasions above), breaking up of a family is thoroughly discouraged. It is strongly believed that the family is the most foundational cohesive element in a society. Persistent, patient (even if prolonged) counseling is a very important duty of this association. This method and practice of intensive and extensive counseling, instead of strictly enforcing "Do"s and "Don't"s, (as found in the patriarchy bound societies) may fail inspite of best intentions and endeavours. But, the Association does not feel demoralised. Its rewards are in its sincere endeavours. The State, through its designated Welfare Officers, takes over the responsibility and is usually successful.

The second major duty and preoccupation of these associations is to untiringly organise meetings, fasts, rallies and protest demonstrations. The spirit of patriotism can never be allowed to become weak.

A rather pertinent question that comes automatically into the mind is why particularly a *Women's* association for the purpose of organising the refugees for their freedom struggle,...why not a common association? Was it in recognition to the fact that women (though nuns mostly) were quite in the forefront of the struggle against the initial PRC occupation of Tibet?...I could not really manage a probable answer to this.

One very important thing that we must keep in mind is that we must not commit the folly of oversimplifying and over glorifying this society. It is strikingly gender equal no doubt, but the level of consciousness is not equal among all. It varies from individual to individual, family to family, and settlement to settlement. Quite a good majority of the housewives, with low literacy and low income levels, are not too conscious of or concerned about what happens to the women and what exactly should be happening to them. They are neither too happy nor disturbed about their state of life or lifestyle. Nor are they much worried or sad about their refugee status or living in a foreign country.... The associations serve a very necessary and effective role in this regard.It gives lot of moral support and impetus to the women refugees which, in turn, invigorates the entire community and nation.

References

1. *Dalai Lama, Tibet, China & the World: a compilation of interviews.* (Nartheng Publications, Dharamshala, H.P.) 1989.
2. John Strattan Hawley (ed.), *Fundamentalism and Gender* (OUP, New York, 1994).
3. *Ibid and Facts About Tibet* (Tibetan Youth Congress, 1993).
4. (1) Tibetan Women, (2) Tibetan Women Today (3) Women of Tibet (China Intercontinental Press) and (4) my interviews conversations etc. with hundreds of Tibetan women of all ages and occupation.
5. *Ibid.*

8

Perceiving The Society As An Overall Experience And Experiment

A. Non-violence and peace i.e. peace with Nature, with neighbours or the people around, including the non-Tibetans, with all classes and categories of people and, above all, peace with the opposite sex, is the most basic of the basic characteristics of the society under study. "Peace with the opposite sex is a formidable challenge in any other society.

B. The highest emphasis (of this society) is on non-violence to and peace with Nature or the Environment around. Violence to Nature or to the natural & human environment around us is tantamount to violence against oneself. If we cut a tree to make our house and furniture, we are becoming the cause of less oxygen, less rainfall and less retention power of the soil. We are thus, also infringing into the habitat of not only the wild animals, but also of the human dwellers of the forest; we are taking away their food and livelihood. They are, therefore, forced to migrate.

Along with their food and livelihood, their songs, dances, lifestyle the culture itself is getting robbed. The animals start dying due to starvation and poaching, and the Nature gets into terrible imbalance. The Tibetan Constitution is the only known Constitution that has an exclusive section on environment and its conservation. Abuse or destruction of Nature, in any form or degree, is considered as serious a criminal offence as abuse & destruction of human life and dignity. The belief is that human beings are as much an essential part of Nature as the trees and the animals are and that Nature is as much a part of human civilizations as science, industries and other developmental forces are.

The degeneration in the quality of human life starts simultaneously and inevitably with the destruction of Nature. The modern man, "bestowed with industrial & technological marvels", cannot really live without the gift of Nature. From where will his food, water and the production and construction material come? The industries ,too, survive on the raw materials coming from the ever bountiful Nature.

C. The Tibetans' system of medicine is based totally on the herbs and minerals available locally, i.e. in the Himalayas. They shear the wool for their clothes no doubt, but leaving enough for the sheep to protect itself from cold. The dye used is purely natural from tea leaves, turmeric, indigo, tobacco, "kattha" ,etc.,for example. Their love for Nature and the commitment to preserve it is so strong that they changed their food habit. This is most difficult for any cultural group to achieve. While in Tibet, they concentrated on animal food because in that cold desert there was very little possibility for agriculture. In India they have adapted to the local food habit with amazing ease and eagerness. The change, they felt, was necessary because of the local climatic conditions also.

D. This quality to adapt easily and eagerly can also be ascribed as the reason behind taking to a dramatically different socio-political system without any protests or grievances. The new democratic Constitution (or the legal system) for a classless, gender-equal socio-economic structure, that is how, got actually implemented (and did not remain merely on paper as it is in India or in similar civilizations).

E. The newly-adopted and eagerly accepted socio-political system also fits perfectly well with their love for Nature and everything natural. Nobody can deny that all homo sapiens were born equal (except with regard to their bone structures, skin colours, texture of hairs and facial features) and that all the existing differences and discriminations were invented /created by those who wanted to be in power. It is needless to remind and reiterate that power's birthplace is differentiation, division, discrimination, deprivation and, finally, destruction of the identity of the overpowered or the ruled. Nature thrives and survives on perfect balance and harmony. Lovers of Nature, therefore, cannot believe in or practise inequality.

It is important to investigate, at this point, why socio-economic stratification existed in traditional Tibet and why the Tibetan rulers became so conscious of the value of equality only after leaving their traditional geo-climatic and cultural base?! In that case is it a boon in disguise that they had to be "uprooted"?...But then, why similar social transformation does not take place in case of so many other trans-national migrants? Before attempting an answer to this query we must keep in mind that no other migrant/ refugee nation ever got the benefit of being allowed to form a government of its own. Migrants, generally, face hostility & alienation from the host nation.

F. The Tibetans of Darjeeling claim that the inspiration behind the Constitution of the Tibetan government in-Exile is their own egalitarian society, which got established over a period of many imperceptibly generations. May be this claim or belief is not wrong. But, what then are the reasons behind this kind of transformation in that society?...The answers are not known. The numerous such women (I mean those who had migrated quite a few generations ago and are Indian citizens) I met during my field study in the Darjeeling district do not have an answer to this. They were born and brought up in *such* an egalitarian society; so they thought this was natural. They are not oblivious about the "unequal" Hindu society. Yet,they did not realise, till questioned by me, that their social structure was so different as to attract so much of attention, interest and admiration. In fact, my questions and interviews made them conscious of their "unique" socio-legal system. They had never given it a thought. My inquiries set them to thinking....I, too, leave this question open to all my readers.

G. "Buddhism", can be another possible answer. Buddhism is not a religion as it does not talk of God and the associated "Do's" & "Dont's". There is no concept of a super-power or a fear in the super-natural powers. It is ethics, based on Buddha's preachings for a moral life and humane beliefs. The notions of the "superior" and the " all powerful" are missing in this "ism". So the institutions of inequality, dominance and oppression are likely not to be there. Sri Lanka, situated geographically in the same cultural belt, has less unequal social structure, it is believed, because of Buddhism. But, then what about the societies of China and Japan, for example? Japan continues to be gender-oppressive and China has changed only after, and as a result of, the Socialist Revolution and the firm implementation of its laws and policies.

Besides, the Sri Lankan society is not as egalitarian as the Tibetan society in exile is....Within Hindu India there are various levels of caste and gender inequalities and some of the tribal (adivasi) cultural patterns show encouraging levels of gender equality.

H. In that case should we ascribe this egalitarianism to the "socialist" reforms in Tibetan Autonomous Region? The reforms were introduced, with revolutionary speed, in 1951 itself. The Tibetans migrated en masse, after more than 8 years, only when and only because their unquestioned and unquestionable spiritual-cum-temporal leader, the Dalai Lama, decided to seek shelter in India. Can the possibility of the Chinese "revolution" penetrating into the cracks of an archaic socio-economic structure be totally ruled out? The powerless, viz: the serfs and the women, would have naturally welcomed it. The thesis that the feudal lords and the officials decided to engineer a mass "flight in distress" because they wanted to save their face before they lose their power and status completely cannot also be totally disowned.

True freedom and equality go hand in hand; they can be interpreted as synonymous terms and concepts. The new-found freedom from the bondage of feudal land holding coupled with the educational & other opportunities for the common people opened their eyes to the supreme truth that equality only can help them retain this long-desired freedom.

They may have had tasted this freedom and some kind of equality in the new Tibet under PRC and thus developed a willingness for it. The Dalai Lama is too wise & pragmatic not to have noticed this sentiment among his people. His training in the Western liberal education system must have also made him realise that the new Tibet (in exile) needs to be re-moulded. Very seldom has human history seen such a wise and people-centric leader.

It is not possible to ascertain the validity of such assumptions since we get totally contradictory reports from the Tibetan Women's Association on the one hand and the Chinese government sources,on the other. But, conversations with a few Tibetan girls, who had come to India on a temporary visit (to learn English better, in most of the cases) from TAR tends to convert our assumptions into facts. The video film made by an apolitical Indian (I mentioned about it earlier) also disproves most of the allegations made by the Tibetan activists. I got encouraging news about the actual situation in TAR and the conditions of the ordinary citizens in "China-occupied" Tibet from those Tibetans who keep receiving letters from their friends and relatives who have opted to stay back. I also spoke to those who keep visiting their friends and relatives in India on and often. These Tibetans start speaking spontaneously, without being conscious of what they are expected to speak in a situation where their fellow Tibetans in exile are constantly fighting a battle for the liberation of the land from where they were "forced" to flee. All these "visitors" from Tibet know their mother tongue well, contrary to the propaganda by the Tibetan government machineries in India. They also know the language of the Han Chinese. But their English is not good and they come to India mainly to learn English. Tibetan Women's Association Reports insist that Tibetan language is not being taught in TAR.

When asked about the repressions in Tibet, these young girls (either school or early college going) took a bit of time to comprehend the question. That showed that repressions or oppressions, if any, were not too pronounced or intolerable. Or, may be, in so many years they have got so used to that these no longer strike them as something objectionable or unacceptable.

Some of them do talk of absence of religious freedom, but they do not appear to be hooked on to religion the way the Tibetan activists in India are. They are deeply religious the way the Prophets or the essence of any religious thought would like one genuine follower to be. They are not fanatics. The ethics or the universal moral principles guide them and bind them to the true values of a human life. Religious philosophy is more or less the same or similar in all religions.

There can be no denying the fact (at the same time), that the Tibetans in India are attached to their lamas, monasteries and the highest spiritual leader with deep emotions. Their mundane life and thinking are intricately inter-twined with their moral-cum-spiritual.

I. I happened to be in Kalimpong, the oldest known Tibetan settlement in India, on the very auspicious occasion of the full moon that comes immediately after Lord Buddha's birthday. It was a very important religious festival and a cherished occasion for community gathering. All their festivals are religion based and occasions for the entire community to leave all jobs and busy-ness. They exchange queries, informations and pleasantries. This is quite similar to the Bengali tradition of Durga puja, which is a full-fledged cultural get-together in the name of a religious ritual. Thus, it was a golden opportunity for me to meet, observe and talk to men and women of all ages, occupations, ideas and beliefs.

Each and every men & women, were extremely warm and forthcoming. They were happy to find somebody so closely interested in their society. What made them happier is that I already knew quite a bit about their society and have long association with it. They even stopped their religio-cultural programmes for an hour or so because they wanted to hear me and ask me questions. I spoke in Hindustani with as many Nepali words I could remember from my childhood days. The local language, Nepali is the lingua franca with the pre-1959 Tibetans, who enjoy Indian citizenship and psychologically feel completely rooted in the Indian eco-political ethos.

J. Not all of them felt elated with the show of BJP-ruled India's enemy-combat capabilities viz: the bomb explosion at Pokharan. They were quite unlike the refugee Tibetans I met at Delhi, Dharamshala and Shimla. The majority of the women and the school children appeared keen for *peaceful* relations with India's neighbours. They were more concerned about their life in the land they have been living since many generations (more than a century in case of quite a number of families) than about a dream, viz: the liberation of Tibet. Tibet,to them, is merely a land for cultural inspiration. Inspite of amicable relations with the local and other Indians, these Tibetans have all the same remained stuck emotionally to their culture and religion.

Yet, they do not think of going back to Tibet. Their memories of Tibet are not all that beautiful. Their fore-fathers had left a feudal Tibet where the serfs and women were unfree, although far less oppressed than it was in a typical European feudalism or under Indian zamindari and caste system. Luckily for them, they have managed to evolve a socio-economic system in their new habitat which has turned out to be extremely beneficial. They do not know how and when exactly this happened. The present generation of women and the girl children that I met are so used to this system that they could not think of a reason behind this equality and freedom. They were,in fact, greatly surprised with my query. It is not that they have not observed the inequalities and the gender discriminations amongst their friends' families, but they thought the Indian social system is different because it is different in so many other ways also. It did not occur to them that their own society is an innovation being unique and different from their society that existed in Tibet.

K. One important point has to be made here. The population composition of the "Indian" society in this part of West Bengal is more non-Indian, racially and culturally—a majority are Lepchas, Gurkhas, Bhutias,etc. Their patriarchal structures are much less oppressive. The wonder of wonders is the Marwari trading community here! Their women have been allowed to become as educated and as modern as the Nepali and the Tibetan women around. They are not exploitative like their kins in Calcutta or other areas of mainstream India. Is it the result of interactions with the Tibetans for generations? The Tibetans had originally (as mentioned earlier) come to this part of India to trade and these Marwaris were the ones they originally interacted with. As far back as our knowledge and their memory extend, these interactions were friendly. These interactions and relations must have been to the advantage of the Tibetan traders. Life here must have been fruitful and more livable. That is why they decided to stay back.

They made me put "scarves of reverence" to the life-size photographs of the Dalai Lama and the Panchen Lama and also put such scarves around my neck. I received scarves, warmth and full co-operation whenever I addressed meetings, organised quickly and efficiently by the local administration and the women' associations. Comfortable, homely stay in hotels run by Tibetan families were arranged. These are the places where I saw how the entire family of three to four generations work together in perfect gender and generation harmony. The husband and wife cook together and their children run small errands and serve the customers while reading school books and writing their home assignments. The father-in-law also cooks and serves if the other members (of the family) are busy or sick or tired. Sometimes, he prefers cooking because he happens to be a better cook. The mother-in law almost always takes over all the tiring household chores when the daughter-in-law is pregnant or nursing. The husband does all these if his mother is a little too old or not well. I have noticed women mostly selling woollens and men helping her in various ways. The father-in-law & daughter-in-law entrepreneurship in the eating joints is quite a common sight.

L. When asked why they want to go back to Tibet, leaving such a gender-equal society which they got as a gift in exile, the refugee women find it difficult to come out with an answer about which they are convinced. On the other hand, a majority of them, who are Indian citizens, do not really understand my question. They find such a question quite uncalled for because they fail to accept that their society or status here is so different, attracting so much of attention. They find their society quite natural and nothing unusual. They are born and brought up in this and therefore, are so very used to it. There was never an occasion or reason for them to think or feel that they are so different and striking! Besides, they have no clear idea about the society in Tibet, which the "late-comers" or the post-1959 migrants have been "forced" to leave. Their confusion increases when the activists or the Women's Associations talk of going back to that land. They wonder why should anybody or a woman particularly, like to go back to a land where,it is said, there was no freedom for women and the common people. The freedom fighters cannot be insane or fools... That is why, they find it difficult to believe or agree that the society in their motherland was not gender and class equal.

Freedom of one's own land from foreign interference is indisputedly the goal of any nation and to start living again in one's own land has to be its strong desire. Patriotism is a highly idealised emotion and has to be necessarily unquestioning. Under this idealism "motherland" or territory becomes sacred and tends to get its place above people, their needs and even their culture and tradition!...This can be a dangerous trend under certain socio-political combinations — as we find now in India under the Hindutva Parties. The

Tibetan activists, unfortunately, have adopted similar strategies (viz; of the Hindutva protagonists). Common people and even the students are kept ignorant about the nature and history of the Tibetan society before the Chinese aggression. They are told only about the tortures and oppressions and the throttling of the religious rights as a result of this aggression; they are never told about the feudal and monastic oppressions in the pre-modern Tibetan polity.

But the high school teachers, academicians and the government officials, including the Private Secretary to the present Dalai Lama, are wise enough not to deny history because they know that a researcher like me must have come well-armed with sufficient knowledge about their society, past and present. They admit the "backwardness" of their "non-democratic" society and polity in "old" Tibet. But they do not consider that ground enough for the Chinese aggression and occupation. They confidently say that they will take this system, which they developed in exile, back to Tibet and they will not allow feudalism and the accompanying inequalities to return. In fact, they believe that democracy will grow further and become stable once the nation is back in its *own* land and environment.

The women, particularly the young girls born in India, are generally evasive about the answers. They either keep quiet or try to divert my attention by asking me counter-questions about my own society. Some of them are genuinely eager to know why and in which all respects the mainstream Indian society is so different from theirs. The present generation looks awe-struck, but the generation of the grandmothers looks lost in trying to revive their memory and relive, as if, their experiences. An animated discussion or exchange of ideas start among themselves and spontaneously they start narrating their experiences and feelings, quite excitedly, to each other and finally, through an interpreter, to me. Most of them are uneducated and do not know any other language except Tibetan.

Interestingly, so many of them had not realised, till that moment, that their society in Tibet had been relatively inegalitarian and oppressive. Side by side, they wonder why 50 long years of independence and democratic Constitution could not do to the Indian society what their own democratic Constitution did in just a few years or almost instantaneously. After all, the Constitution of the Tibetan Government in Exile has been inspired by India's Constitution only! Once again, they felt grateful to the Indian government for offering them the right avenues to democracy, viz: education and health. Till they availed of these benefits they had not realised how important education and health are for any individual group or nation. They had not realised that freedom comes through this path and no power can stop this process once it is on.

This valuable realisation, on account of the Tibetan "experience" in India, positively intervened into my thought process and I understood what was the motive behind our government doing the least in the fields of health and education. The best way to maintain power is to perennially keep the "ruled" backward so that they can never raise their heads and question the whims of the authority. This is the reason why the male Parliamentarians in India are up in arms against the possibility of women coming to almost equal power in the highest law-making and decision-taking body. And, the absence of this mentality is the reason why women's representation in the Tibetan Parliament is almost equal *without any reservation*. (I have discussed this at an earlier place.)

Another striking feature of the Tibetan mentality and attitude is that they make maximum of the opportunities and try untiringly to create new ones for themselves. At the same time, they are not greedy or overambitious. Like all hill and tribal people they get contented easily; they do not hanker after more and more at the cost of the legitimate share of the others. But, they are not easily content with their own capabilities and the endless possibilities. This characteristic is slightly more pronounced with the girls and the women.

I found higher level of motivation and seriousness among the children of those who are Indian citizens and therefore, are eligible for the Indian government jobs. They are interested in Indian and world politics like any other Indian. They are more concerned about India's border problems and her domestic policies than about Tibet becoming free of Chinese occupation. They do not like the ruling Left Front in Bengal because they agree with the Nepalis that the hills have been badly neglected. They are not also happy with the BJP and the Pokharan blasts.

But, BJP is a hot favourite with the refugees and with a few highly educated Indian Tibetans because this Party has taken a consistent anti-China stand. At the same time, they cannot help feeling greateful to the Congress Party for what the first Prime Minister of India (from this Party) had done for them. They feel grateful to his daughter also.

There is also a large group of Indian Tibetans

who are happy with the Left parties because of their commitment to the cause of class and gender equality. They find the social beliefs and attitudes of the BJP rather obnoxious. But the Tibetans of other settlements have no notion of the ideology of the Left parties and they are very happy with BJP because of its belligerent stand towards PRC. Unlike the naturalised "Indian" Tibetans, their entire consciousness is overshadowed by their determination to go back to their own land somehow or other, some day or other. Unlike again, they do not have the feeling of oneness with India and the Indians, however grateful they may be for the asylum and all the benefits they are enjoying. They have remained isolated from mainstream India because of their education in the exclusive atmosphere of through the Tibetan Central Schools. The "Indian" Tibetans go to any school along with the other Indians. The former's mindset could have been different—similar to the Indian Tibetans if they had opportunities toget educated in the normal Indian schools. They can get jobs only in their own government offices thus, once again, losing the opportunity to mingle up and interact with the mainstream Indians. They get limited opportunities to know the Indians, since a majority of them live and interact within a specified political territory given over to them by the Govt. of India.

M. In Darjeeling intermixing among the various racio-cultural groups like the Sikkimese, Bhutias, Nepalis, is so perfect that culturally they tend to acquire each other's characteristics. As mentioned earlier, Nepali is the lingua franca and all Tibetans understand and speak Nepali and quite a few non-Tibetans also understand Tibetan. Intermarriages, though discouraged, are not all that uncommon because love-marriages are becoming more and more common. Such marriages are discouraged because the older generation feels that it is unfair to expect from the spouses from other religions to adapt to the Tibetan norms and rituals. A Tibetan family, however modern and progressive, is never agreeable to giving up its religious customs and rites.

Tibetan and Sikkimese women are quite often mistaken for each other because of their identical dress, similar looks and intermarriages. Quite a few Sikkimese women identify themselves as Tibetans and work for Tibet's freedom because they get benefits viz: money and recognition that way. Sometimes they are genuinely confused about their identities because of liberal and spontaneous intermingling. Cases (very few though) of a Tibetan marrying a mainstream Indian (say a Punjabi or an Assamese) and even an Indian Chinese have been found.

Religion to them is not merely a way of life, but also "dharma", i.e. "something that holds", in the truest sense of the term. Wherever they go to, whatever they do and whatever is their path of thinking, their mind and way of life can never be detracted from what Buddha said or what the Dalai Lama now says. That is why their society is almost totally free of any crime. Once in a while there may be a murder or two in the heat of an emotion, but never stealing or disgracing women.

As mentioned above, the activists and the emotionally charged refugees are a bit unhappy with the non-refugee Tibetans. They find them not patriotic enough. The Indian Tibetans, on the other hand, consider the post-1959 migrants "fanatics" & "exclusivists". Quite a few of them have secretly disclosed to me that they have no intention of going back to Tibet even if it becomes free someday, because Tibet is just a concept and not a reality for them. They are deeply rooted in, where they are living for decades and generations. They would not like to go to any other part of India even, not to speak of any other part of the world. They do not also want to give up any part of the culture they have acquired and got assimilated into slowly over a considerable period of time and history. Thirdly they have nothing to gain in the "liberated" Tibet because that will not be able to offer them anything more or better. They had achieved long, long back what the new Tibetan government in Tibet can be hoped bring about. They have now come to know, to their great surprise and delight, that their "age-old" social pattern & structure became a model for the new society in exile and is a dream for all who are struggling endlessly for equal rights & freedom for women and girl children.

N. It is important to highlight at this juncture the rationale behind the need and the formation of Women's Associations. Usually women come together to fight oppression and inhuman discriminations; but those features are missing in this society. The role of the members or the activists is mainly (i) to keep the mood and the momentum of the freedom struggle alive. Women are considered to be more serious, more committed and more motivated in whatever they do or decide to do. This is very much true in case of the Indian sub-continent also. India would not have had the dubious distinction of having the highest number of illiterates in the world in 2000 A.D. if women were allowed to actively participate in the policy-making and implementations in the fields of health and education—the most vital for true, people-centric, development. (ii) The second important work that the Associations do is to offer counseling to couples and families in dispute.

But the value of such associations is more importantly in the following truths—

1. Women are the better custodians of environment and culture. We do not need to go into the details of the argument as this is a well-known and well-accepted fact all over the world and particularly, in the Indian subcontinent.

2. Women are mothers and it is a well-acclaimed fact that mothers are the primary and the best teachers. That is the reason why all social workers believe that women should be fully educated, emancipated and with a scientific temperament.

3. Women can influence the minds and mould the convictions more effectively. And that definitely can serve the cause of the new society and the freedom struggle better. Forgiving, understanding and counseling are the most striking features of a Tibetan character in general; and these are more easily found in women as compared to men. Exceptions, of course, can be in every society, including the Tibetan.

Conclusion

I had stared writing this book as an extension of my longstanding concern for the migrants and refugees. The migration or homelessness can be within a political set up (like in case of the adivasis from Jharkhand or other areas of "developing" India) or from across an international border (like in case of the Afghans, the Burmese or the Tibetans who fled from the "onslaught" of a new/ different eco-political order). My deep interest is primarily because I regard the migrations of communities (en bloc) as the unavoidable consequences of the autocratic belief of a few in power that "I/We are superior to you and therefore, I/We know best what is good for you". The adivasis of the Narmada valley are forced to leave their home and livelihood just because others have usurped the right to decide what is good for them. They may even have to give up their lives one day ! The peace-loving, ever contented people of Tibet had to traverse miles of hardship from the other side of the Himalayas just because developing China felt that it was her duty, as a peoples' government, to spread the benefits of modern development far and wide. In both the cases, the political authorities did not care to know what *really* is *people's* good, and whether the *people* understand and accept that the nature and mode of *development* are for their good.

That is why, all "developmental" activities within a capitalist framework and a totalitarian political ideology have, inevitably, led to the destruction of a people's identity & the people's faith in the system. Migration thus, is the only alternative left in the hands of the people, looking, in vain though, for a new "home" and a new identity. So, anger against power wrested by a few and concern for those who were rendered powerless, had originally prompted me into this kind of work.

In pre-history, civilizations grew/ prospered as a result of trade, cultural exchange, various other interactions and even migrations and consequent assimilations in the new civilizations. Such migrations and assimilations were totally voluntary. That helped the migrants to flower and prosper and not get dispossessed and destroyed (like it is now in almost all the cases). As I delved deeper and deeper into the problem and came to know viz: the Tibetan exiles, better and better, I found myself in the most curious position of changing my, (or the established), views about the effects of migration or the transplantation of a cultural group on a new soil. The more I came to know this society and the people from a closer and closer angle, I was amazed to discover that the "displacement" in this case has actually done them good. This is a unique society *in exile* which has achieved all that a democratic society/ polity, ideally, wants to achieve. The society is unbelievably devoid of any class or gender division, whatsoever. As I have mentioned a number of times in the chapters earlier, the Tibetans themselves are unaware of this phenomenon,but. This trait has remained unobserved. Strangely, the numerous scholars and the authors of books on this community and society also have failed to make a note of this.

May be this is the advantage of a study from the gender angle. One has to probe into the deepest and the most hidden layers of a society; so all the layers necessarily unfold themselves and the true picture gets revealed.

The end result of this work has given me a level of satisfaction which is difficult to put in words. It is sheer joy and pride. Joy and pride because, as a woman and as a crusader for casteless and classless human civilization, I felt that I have finally reached my Utopia. So, I present this work as a *Model* for gender equality. This can be a model not only for those men in power who talk of equality and pretend helplessness, but even for women who, unwittingly, are trained to accept their inferior and chained status. The former will feel ashamed, the latter will find the courage to question. The very small number of the "empowered". will feel encouraged and more empowered.

Bibliography

1. A.V.Arakeri, *Tibetans in India: The Uprooted People and Their Cultural Transplantation* (Reliance Publishing House, New Delhi), 1998.

2. Ajit Bhattacharya, *Tibetans in Exile: The Democratic Vision* (Tibetan Parliamentary and Policy Research Centre, New Delhi), 1994.

3. The Dalai Lama, *Tibet, China And The World*: A Compilation of interviews. (Narthang Publications, Dharamshala (H.P.),1989.

4. Prof. Samdhong Rinpoche (Chairman, Assembly of Tibetan People's Deputies), *Tibet:A Future Vision* (Tibetan Parliamentary and Policy Research Centre), 1996.

5. *Life in Exile* (Central Tibetan Relief Committee, Dept. of Home, Dharamshala (H.P.),1992.

6. *Tibet's Parliament in Exile*. (Tibetan Parliamentary and Policy Research Centre),1996.

7. *Tibetan Women: Oppression* and *Discrimination in Occupied Tibet*; National Report on Tibetan Women (issued by the Tibetan Administration in Dharamshala,

India for The Fourth World Conference on Women, Beijing),1995.

8. *Tibetan Bulletin* (the official journal of the Tibetan Administration—a quarterly), all the issues of 1996-98.

9. *Tibetan Women*, (China Intercontinental Press).

10. *Tibetan Women Today* (China Intercontinental Press).

11. *Women of Tibet* (China Intercontinental Press).

12. Dawa Norbu, *Red Star Over Tibet.*

13. K. Booth & M. Tienda, *Migration, Gender* and *Social Change*; A Review and Reformulation. (Paper presented at a UN conference on this theme in June, 1988 at Oslo).

14. K. Hart, *Rural-Urban Migration.* (in "The Journal of Modern African Studies",vol.II, from Cambridge, New York).

15. *Unesco, History of Humanity*, vol. 3. 1996.

16. Alex Wayman, *Untying The Knots in Buddhism.* (Motilal Banarsidass Publishers, Delhi), 1997.

17. Ananda K. Coomaraswamy & I.B. Harner, *The Living Thoughts of Gotama, The Buddha.*, (London, 1948).

18. I.B. Harner, Women under Primitive Buddhism. (Motilal Banarsidass, Delhi),1975.

19. A.C.Bouquet, *Sacred Books of The World.* (Cassel, London),1962.

20. G.B.Upreti, *Early Buddhist World Outlook in Historical Perspective*, Calcutta,1998.

21. Kunzang Lama'i Shelung (translated by Patrul Rinpoche), *The Words of My Perfect Teacher.* (Harper Collins Publishers, India.) 1996.

22. Ven. Pategama Gnanarama, *An Approach to Buddhist Social Philosophy.* (Ti-Sarana Buddhist Association,

Appendix 1

Questionnaire Used with the Tibetans in Exile, at Dharamshala, Shimla, Delhi

1. When did you come to India? Before or after 1951, 1959 ?
2. Did you come with His Holiness?
3. Did you, like most migrants, come Darjeeling?
4. Did you, like most migrants, study in Darjeeling?
5. What is your education/vocational trainning?
6. When & why did you come to Dharamshala/Delhi/ Shimla?
7. What is your family & marital status?
8. What is your occupation/income?
9. What is your husbands/father's/brother's occupation?
10. What is your husband's/brother's/ income?
11. How many children you have ? What are they doing?

12. How many brothers & sisters you have/had. What are they doing?

13. What all work your husband does at home? Do you have specific division of labour or you share all the work?

14. Do your children, specially sons, help you or do household work?

15. Do you train/encourage your children/sibbings in household work ? Did your mother do the same ?

16. Does your husband ask/encourage children, particularly sons, to do household work ?

17. How is your and husband's income shared or spent ? What role you have in decisions regarding (i) money, (ii) property, (iii) children ?

18. What is your role as a mother ? Do you have equal right to decide about number of children, their bringing up and your sexual life ?

19. How do men and your society think of women's role as daughter, wife and mother and their responsibility towards their families and society ?

20. How do men and your society think of women's sexuality and what type of crimes against women are prevalent in your society ?

21. Do you feel better-off here, in India ?

22. What is the main reason why you want to go back to Tibet ? Why are you unhappy here ?

Appendix 2

Questionnaire Used with Tibetan Women in the Darjeeling District

Considering the special chracteristic of the Tibetans settled in the Darjeeling district (of W. Bengal)—as explained in my project proposal and subsequent discussions — I asked the following questions, in addition to the questions (which have been used for those who have migrated to India after 1959.

1. When...... how many generations back.... did your family/forefathers come to Darjeeling?
2. Did he come alone, in the beginning, or with his family?
3. When did he *settle down* in Darjeeling? Did he come to Darjeeling straight from Tibet *or* from any other part of India, or from Nepal/Bhutan/Sikkim ?
4. What was the main reason why he came and settled down outside his motherland?
5. Have you learnt from your forefathers about the socio-economic condition of Tibet when he migrated?

(a) What was the socio-economic condition, particularly of women.... your mother's your grandmother's etc.... (i) in Tibet and (ii) in Darjeeling (India) at that time?

(b) What level of education did they have in (i) Tibet and (ii) in India?

(c) What economic opportunities did they have in (i) & (ii)?

(d) What kind of freedom or decision-making powers they had with regard to (i) property & income (ii) marriage/sex and (iii) children?

(e) What was their marital status?

6. What kind of socio-economic status, job and education opportunities and decision-making powers you have ? The sub-divisions of questions will be similar to Q 5.

7. Did your forefather or you go to Tibet after 1951? If yes, what impression you have about TAR ? Do you agree with the post 1959 migrants about the PRC oppression and loss of freedom there?

8. What kind of relations you have with the local Indians and Gurkhas ? Do they treat you in the same manner as they treat the post 1959 settlers?

9. What kind of relations you have with post 1959 settlers? Do you get the same benefits from the Indian and Dalai Lama Govt.-in-exile as they get?

10. Do you think life (socio-economic situation) is better for you now, after the establishment of Tibetan govt.-in-exile? In what all ways?

11. Do you intend to return to Tibet? If "yes", why?

Appendix 3

Interviewing Lohsang Teinpfa & Tenzin Geyche, P.S. to H. H. Dalai Lama

1. Since when are you working with His Highness? (a) Did you come to India with him? (b) Earlier? (c) Latter?
2. Educational Qualifications?

   Age ?
3. Anybody left behind?

   If so, why?

   Any communication with them?

   What do they write about present status in "occupied Tibet" ?
4. Have you ever visited PRC?

   your impressions?
5. Frankly, is there any economic development in Tibet due to "occupation"?

6. What was the socio-economic condition of Tibet & its people before you migrated?
7. What, in (i) your, (ii) other migrants & (iii) H.H's eyes the present socio-economic condition in Tibet?
8. Is socio-economic condition better/worse in India?

   If better, why? In what respects?

   If worse, why (frankly)?
9. How are you viewed & treated by

   (i) local people

   (ii) Indians, in general

   (iii) Government of India?
10. Do (i) climate, (ii) natural vegetation & medicinal herbs, (iii) food have any role in Tibetans wanting to go back home?
11. Why is it that a good no of Tibetans had already migrated to India, Sikkam, Nepal, etc even before the PRC attack?
12. Why the Tibetan migrants do not join hands with the other political. migrants like the Burmese, Palestinians and (earlier) Bangladeshis?
13. What are the reason behind PRC occupation?

Appendix 4

Questionnaire for Scholars on Chinese Studies

1. Tibetan history and the Tibetans claim that Tibet was always *sovereign and independent*, and PRC grabbed it in 1951. But British Raj and a school in India think Tibet definitely was an autonomous region, but not a sovereign state what is the real story?

2. Since Marxism and Maoism are basically fights against oppression and, therefore, against all form of imperialism and since PRC has helped many nations struggling for their freedom, do you think PRC could have allowed the Tibetans freedom or at least, autonomy?

3. Quite a strong world opinion, particularly in the western industrialised world, has been created in favour of the struggle and demands of the Tibetans both in Tibet and in exile. What do you think is/are the reasons behind this "moral support" to the Tibetan's cause?

4. A large number of literature and audio-visuals not

only by the affected Tibetans, but even by the Western sympathisers—has sprung up—all describing, in details, the tortures, cultural oppression and politically unfavourable conditions that now prevail in "PRC-occupied" Tibet Do you believe that all those are propaganda or sentimental lies?

5. What was the *real* reason why PRC decided to *spread its political and cultural influence* (which the Tibetans and a large world opinion term as "occupation") to Tibet ? Was it (i) mere demographic adjustment, (as propagated by the supporters of Tibet) or was it (ii) altruistic motive of providing the benefits of "development" and modern industrial civilisation to this "backward" area which believed strongly in the values of tradition including feudalism, conservation of natural environment spiritualism?

6. What is the thinking/belief/feeling of the *Chinese citizens* about (i) PRC position in Tibet, (ii) the feelings and beliefs of the Tibetans about PRC action and (iii) about what the Tibetans are now demanding?

7. Now H.H. Dalai Lama and the Tibetan Parliament in exile have come down to demanding *autonomy only*, i.e. independence in the field of culture, religion and environment conservation, but PRC's hold over defence and foreign affairs, can't there now be an amicable settlement?

8. What, in your opinion, is the cause behind such a perfectly democratic Constitution of the Tibetan Government-in-Exile and such a wonderfully egalitarian system in the new society?

Appendix-5

'Living' Buddha Reaches Reting

The two-year-old seventh reincarnation of the Reting "living" Buddha has arrived at the Reting monastery after completing the formalities in Lhasa, an official report said.

A ceremony to mark the arrival was held in Lhunzhub country on Friday in accordance with religious rituals, Xinhua news agency reported late Saturday night.

It is the first time the boy has seen the Reting monastery, the traditional seat of Reting living Buddhas, after he was officially recognised by the Chinese Government on January 16.

The child's ordination took place in front of a statue of Sakyamuni, known as the founder of Buddhism, inside the Johkang temple in Lhasa, capital of the Tibet Autonomous Region in south-west China.

The formal enthronement will be held in the future,the State-run news agency said.

The Reting Lama holds one of the highest-ranking positions in Tibetan Buddhism after the Dalai Lama, who is in India in exile.

View of His Holiness, the Dalai Lama

What is Lamaism?

Tibetan Lamaism is the predominant religion of Tibet and Mongolia. It is essentially Buddhism of the Mahayana or theistic school, with influences from Shivaism and native ritualistic Shamanism.

In AD 747, the Buddhist monk and scholar Padmasambhava ("born of the lotus") travelled from northern India to Tibet, where he established the first order of lamas, or monks, or superiors. Thereafter, the religion began to develop and spread rapidly.

Who is the supreme leader?

The Lamaic religion is organised according to a traditional hierarchy. The supreme position is occupied by two lamas, the Dalai (Grand) Lama, and the Panchen (The Great Scholar) Lama. The Dalai Lama is the supreme spiritual leader of the followers of Tibetan Buddhism, followed by the Panchen Lama. The title "Panchen" is made up of two syllbles: "Pan (dita)" a Sanskrit word meaning scholar, and "Chen (po)", Tibetan for "great". While the first Dalai Lama and the first Panchen Lama started out as equals, the formal relation between the two was established during the time of the Fifth Dalai Lama who became Tibet's sovereign ruler in 1642. Since then, there has been a tradition of the Dalai Lama "recognising" the successor to the post of Panchen Lama.

The controversy surrounding the appointment of the Eleventh Panchen Lama continues as Gedhun Choeky Nyima, recognised by the 14th Dalai Lama, remains untraced. And Gyaltsen Borbu, the Chinese government's "chosen one", has not been recognised by the Dalai Lama as the reincarnated Lama.

How many sects does Tibetan Buddhism have?

Four: Kagyu, Sakya, Nyingma, and Gelug.

What is the Kagyu tradition?

The Kamtsang of Karma Kagyu tradition was founded by the first Karmapa, Dusum Khyenpa (1110-1193). This tradition, also known as "Black Hat", has remained strong and successful due to an unbroken line of Karmapas, reincarnations of the founder. Tsurphu, in central Tibet, was the main Kagyu monastery until Chinese occupation. In exile, the Kagyu tradition has established its headquarters and principal monastic university at Rumtek in Sikkim. It has opened hundreds of centres across the world. The present head of the Karma Kagyu tradition is H.H.XVII Gyalwa Karmapa Urgyen Drodul Trinley Dorje, duly recognised by the 14th Dalai Lama.

What is the Sakya tradition?

The Sakya tradition is closely linked to the Khon ancestral lineage, derived from "celestial beings". The long lineage has descended from Khon Konchok Gyelpo (1034-1102) founder of the Sakya school. Gyelpo has built a monastery in the Tsang province of central Tibet and named it Sakya, or Grey Earth, monastery. The Sakya tradition has been hereditary since its inception. Ngawang Kunga Theckchen Rinpoche (b. 1945), based in Dehradun, is the 41st occupant of the Sakya Throne.

What is the Nyingma school?

The Nyingma school traces its origins to the Indian adept, Guru Padmasambhava, or Guru Rinpoche as he is popularly known. The principal monastic institutions of the

Nyingma tradition - established in exile - are in Karnataka, Dehradun, Dharamshala and Shimla. The Nyingma tradition is headed by H.H. Penor Rinpoche.

What is the Gelug tradition?

The Gelug tradition was founded by Je Tsongkhapa (1357-1419). Before his death, he handed his Ganden throne to a successor chosen by him, starting a tradition which continues till today. The 99th successor to the Ganden throne, and thus the formal head of the Gelugpa, is Ven. Yeshi Dhondup. The Gelug tradition, which lays emphasis on ethics as expressed through monastic discipline as the basis for religious education and practice, continues to have a dynamic presence in exile. The major Gelug monasteries are located in Karnataka and Arunachal Pradesh.

Index

❑❑❑